DATE DUE

JAN 2 0 2005			
DEC 2 2 2006			

Elements

NITROGEN AND PHOSPHORUS

N P

Grolier Educational

How to use this book

j546
v.11
(2)

This book has been carefully developed to help you understand the chemistry of the elements. In it you will find a systematic and comprehensive coverage of the basic qualities of each element. Each two-page entry contains information at various levels of technical content and language, along with definitions of useful technical terms, as shown in the thumbnail diagram to the right. There is a comprehensive glossary of technical terms at the back of the book, along with an extensive index, key facts, an explanation of the periodic table, and a description of how to interpret chemical equations.

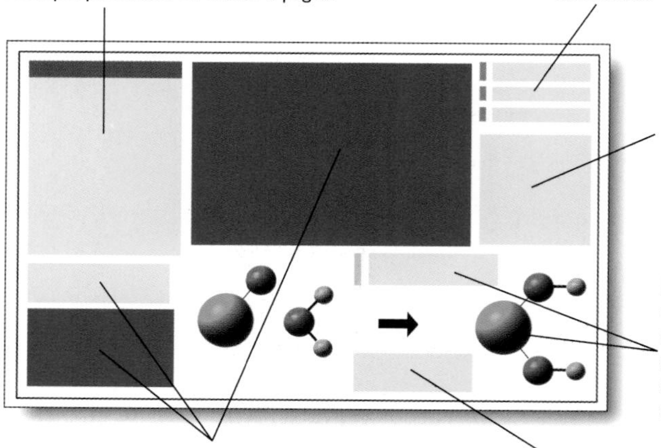
The main text follows the sequence of information in the book and summarizes the concepts presented on the two pages.
Technical definitions.
Substatements flesh out the ideas in the main text with more fact and specific explanation.
Equations are written as symbols and sometimes given as "ball-and-stick" diagrams – see page 48.
Photographs and diagrams have been carefully selected and annotated for clarity.
Also... explains advanced concepts.

Author
Brian Knapp, BSc, PhD
Project consultant
Keith B. Walshaw, MA, BSc, DPhil
(Head of Chemistry, Leighton Park School)
Industrial consultant
Jack Brettle, BSc, PhD (Chief Research Scientist, Pilkington plc)
Art Director
Duncan McCrae, BSc
Editor
Elizabeth Walker, BA
Special photography
Ian Gledhill
Illustrations
David Woodroffe and David Hardy
Electronic page makeup
Julie James Graphic Design
Designed and produced by
EARTHSCAPE EDITIONS
Print consultants
Landmark Production Consultants Ltd
Reproduced by
Leo Reprographics
Printed in Hong Kong by
Wing King Tong Company Ltd

First published in the United States in 1996 by Grolier Educational, Sherman Turnpike, Danbury, CT 06816

First reprint 1997, second reprint 1997, and third reprint 2000. New and revised edition 2002

Copyright © 1996 & 2002
Atlantic Europe Publishing Company Limited

Cataloging information may be obtained directly from Grolier Educational.

Volumes 1-18 Set ISBN: 0–7172–5674–X
Volume 11 ISBN: 0–7172–7583–3
Library of Congress Number: 95–082222
Dewey: 546—dc21

All rights reserved. No part of this publication may be reproduced, stored in a retrieval system, or transmitted in any form or by any means, electronic, mechanical, photocopying, recording, or otherwise, without permission in writing of the publisher.

Acknowledgments
The publishers would like to thank the following for their kind help and advice: *ICI (UK), British Petroleum International* and *Vauxhall Motors Limited.*

Picture credits
All photographs are from the **Earthscape Editions** photolibrary except the following:
(c=center t=top b=bottom l=left r=right)
British Petroleum Company plc 13tl; **ICI** 17tr, 17bl, 21br, 27cr; **NASA** 7tr; **SPL** 18/19, 29br; **Vauxhall Motors Limted** 29t; **Tony Waltham, Geophotos** 28bl and **ZEFA** 7cl, 8/9t, 9br, 21t, 26b.

Front cover: Nitrogen dioxide gas has a characteristic brown color.
Title page: The head of a strike-anywhere match contains a phosphorus compound that ignites with friction. This initiates a reaction of other compounds in the match head.

This product is manufactured from sustainable managed forests. For every tree cut down at least one more is planted.

The demonstrations described or illustrated in this book are not for replication. The Publisher cannot accept any responsibility for any accidents or injuries that may result from conducting the experiments described or illustrated in this book.

Contents

Introduction

An element is a substance that cannot be broken down into a simpler substance by any known means. Each of the 92 naturally occurring elements is therefore one of the fundamental materials from which everything in the Universe is made.

Nitrogen

Nitrogen, chemical symbol N, is a colorless, relatively unreactive (inert) gas without any smell. It is a kind of inert "filler" in our atmosphere, making up over three-quarters of the air we breathe.

The word nitrogen is made up from two Greek words: *nitron*, meaning saltpeter, and *genes*, meaning producing. This is because the most important historic use of nitrogen was as saltpeter, a compound called potassium nitrate, well known since ancient times as a fertilizer.

Nitrogen as a gas is relatively inert, but some nitrogen is also vital to life as part of amino acids, the building blocks of proteins. Thus all living things are made up of compounds including nitrogen, oxygen, hydrogen and carbon. Each of these comes from the air and water around us.

Nitrogen from the air cannot be used directly by plants, so they rely on getting it from soluble nitrogen compounds in the soil.

Each molecule of nitrogen is made up of two nitrogen atoms linked together extremely strongly. Energy is needed to convert the nitrogen (N_2) molecules in the air into nitrogen-

containing compounds. The process of converting the nitrogen is called "fixing." Nature provides two fixing mechanisms. One occurs whenever lightning flashes and heats up the air. Another is through the efforts of the bacteria that live in the nodules of some plant roots (plants called legumes, which include peas, beans and clover). To make use of nitrogen as a fertilizer, people have to dig up rocks containing nitrogen compounds, find chemical ways to make nitrogen compounds or grow legumes in rotation with other plants.

Considerable energy is released when compounds containing nitrogen (N) atoms change and form nitrogen gas (N_2). This is why nitrogen compounds are favored as raw materials for explosives, from gunpowder to nitroglycerine.

Phosphorus

Phosphorus, chemical symbol P, is a solid first obtained from dried urine! It was soon discovered that phosphorus glowed in the dark, and because of this property chemists named the element after the Greek word for "light-bringing."

Quite unlike nitrogen, phosphorus is very reactive and does not exist on its own in nature. On exposure to air, white phosphorus burns spontaneously. However, like nitrogen, phosphorus is known for its use in weapons, in this case because it produces intense flame. Also like nitrogen, phosphorus is essential to life, its compounds helping in the process of transferring energy within the body.

◀ Nitrogen dioxide gas being released by a reaction of fuming nitric acid and copper shavings.

Nitrogen and the atmosphere

Nitrogen is the most abundant gas in the atmosphere, making up 79% by volume and 76% by mass (weight). Nitrogen molecules are bound together so tightly that nitrogen (unlike oxygen) is undisturbed by ultraviolet radiation and is found as gas molecules in the high atmosphere.

Nitrogen was one of the first gases to be formed in the early atmosphere, some four billion years ago. The most likely source was as ammonia gas coming out of volcanoes and hot springs. The ammonia was then acted on by light, breaking down to produce nitrogen and hydrogen.

Over time the other gases of the early atmosphere were partly combined with the Earth's rocks and oceans; or, in the case of hydrogen, they disappeared into space. As a result, the inert nitrogen was left as a greater and greater proportion of the atmosphere.

Nitrogen rarely reacts with the other gases in the atmosphere except at high temperatures during lightning flashes (and in vehicle engines). During a lightning flash, when temperatures reach 30,000°C, nitrogen and oxygen combine to make nitrogen dioxide which, when dissolved in water, makes dilute nitric acid. This is a natural (and modest) source of acid rain. At the same time, it makes nitrogen into soluble products that can be absorbed by plant roots.

Nitrogen as a source of carbon-14

In the upper atmosphere, nitrogen atoms are bombarded by cosmic rays in the form of neutrons. These change the atomic number of the nitrogen, converting nitrogen into radioactive carbon (the carbon isotope carbon-14).

Carbon-14 and oxygen atoms combine to form radioactive carbon dioxide, a gas that is absorbed by plants. In this way tiny amounts of carbon-14 are stored by plants. The residual carbon-14 in carbon-containing materials can be measured to determine the age of the material.

▼ At first the Earth had no atmosphere, but volcanic eruptions slowly produced the gases that make the atmosphere we have today, which is dominated by nitrogen.

► A nitrogen molecule. The three lines joining the two atoms represent a triple bond, which shows that nitrogen has a high "bond energy."

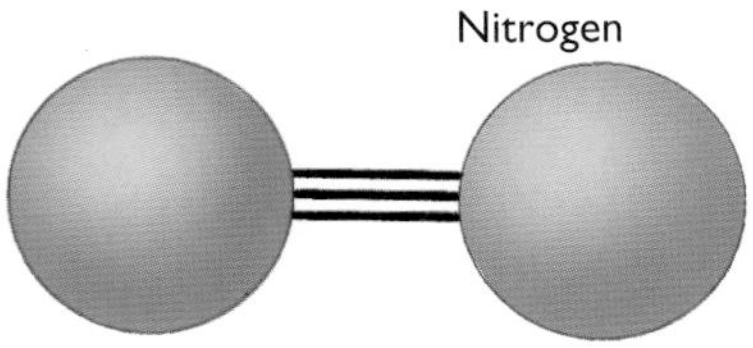

dissolve: to break down a substance in a solution without reacting.

isotopes: atoms that have the same number of protons in their nucleus, but which have different masses; for example, carbon-12 and carbon-14.

radioactive: emitting radiation or particles from the nucleus of its atoms.

Dissolved nitrogen

Nitrogen is readily dissolved in body fluids. The greater the pressure, the more gas is dissolved.

At high altitudes, the pressure of the atmosphere is much less than at ground level and aircraft have their cabins pressurized to provide a comfortable environment. Not only is it essential to provide enough oxygen for breathing, but without this pressure, the levels of nitrogen dissolved in the blood would change quickly, giving rise, as pressures fall, to bubbles of nitrogen forming in the blood and causing the effect that scuba divers call "the bends," which in flying is known as aeroembolism.

▲ Auroras are constantly changing glowing lights seen in the night sky, mainly within the Arctic and Antarctic Circles. Auroras result from an interaction between electrons flowing through space and gases in the upper atmosphere. The auroras may occur as veils, curtains and other shapes. A number of colors are associated with auroras, each reflecting the gas that is being bombarded with electrons. Red colors, produced by the bombarding of nitrogen gas, normally fringe the green colors produced by bombardment of oxygen atoms. This picture shows the red fringe of an aurora as seen from space.

◄ Nitrogen gas is converted to soluble nitrogen dioxide by lightning.

EQUATION: Formation of nitrogen dioxide during lightning flashes

Stage 1: Nitrogen + oxygen ➪ nitric oxide

$$N_2(g) + O_2(g) \Rightarrow 2NO(g)$$

Stage 2: Nitric oxide + oxygen ➪ nitrogen dioxide

$$2NO(g) + O_2(g) \Rightarrow 2NO_2(g)$$

EQUATION: Formation of natural acid raindrops after lightning

Nitrogen dioxide + water ➪ nitric acid + nitric oxide (which can react with more oxygen as above)

$$3NO_2(g) + H_2O(l) \Rightarrow 2HNO_3(aq) + NO(g)$$

"Refining" nitrogen

Nitrogen at normal air pressure and temperature contains so much energy that it is a gas. Nitrogen makes up about three-quarters of the mixture of gases in the atmosphere. However, nitrogen is never found in nature as a liquid or a solid.

Liquid nitrogen

To make nitrogen into a liquid, the gas has to be deprived of energy by cooling. However, this is not very easy because the temperature at which nitrogen liquefies is -196°C.

To make liquid nitrogen easier to obtain, air is cooled while under pressure. You can think of the process as being rather like an air "refinery." Each of the gases in the air has its own condensation point (at which it changes from gas to liquid). As this is reached, the element liquefies. Liquid oxygen forms at -183°C. Nitrogen has the lowest boiling point of any of the gases in the air, and it is the last to be collected.

▼ The composition of clean air.

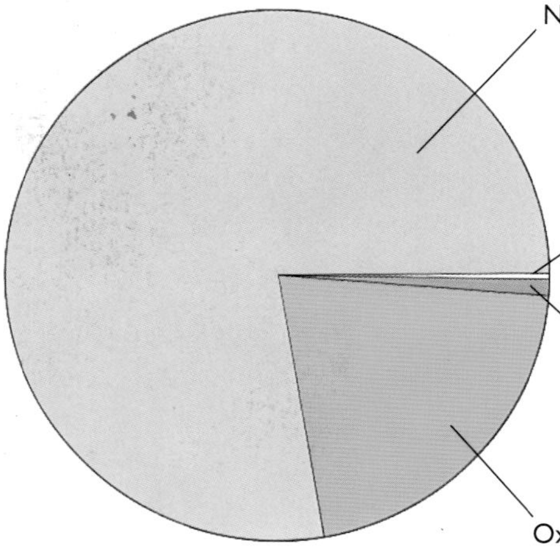
Nitrogen 78%
Carbon dioxide 0.03%
Noble gases 1% (helium, neon, argon, krypton and xenon)
Oxygen 21%

RUSH
DISASSEMBLE PALLETS

Distilling nitrogen

Often the easiest way to obtain nitrogen is to liquefy air in bulk and then allow the oxygen to boil off. This process is called distillation, and it is a very low temperature version of, for example, how oil and other mixtures are obtained from hydrocarbons. The process takes place in a tall column (called a fractionation column) made of a set of "leaky trays." Liquid air is poured onto the trays. There is a boiler at the bottom and a condenser (a trap for the gas given off) at the top.

As the air begins to evaporate, nitrogen is given off as a gas, while the oxygen (which turns into a gas less easily than nitrogen – it is less volatile) drips to the bottom. In this way carefully controlled conditions can separate the nitrogen from the oxygen.

The liquid air is kept under a pressure of five atmospheres in the tower, at which pressure the boiling point of the nitrogen and oxygen are much higher (and so easier to maintain) than at normal atmospheric pressure.

volatile: readily forms a gas.

▲ Nitrogen has many industrial applications. It creates an inert environment for storing experimental samples during research.

► Fractional distillation of air. The liquid air is pumped into a fractionating column and subjected to pressure and temperature changes to separate the component gases that make up air.

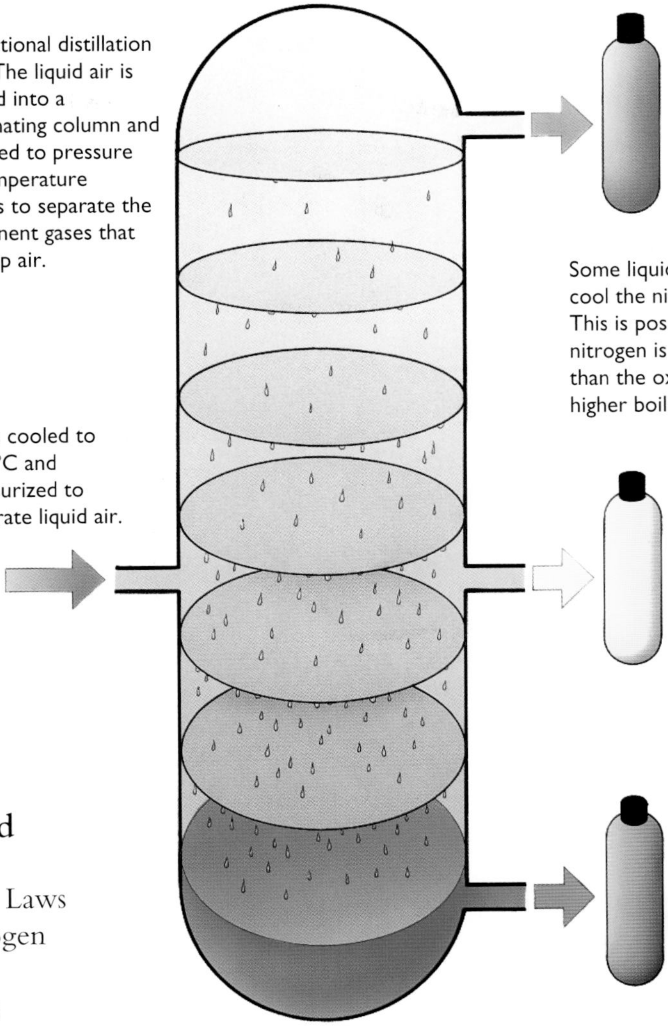
Air is cooled to -190°C and pressurized to generate liquid air.
Nitrogen gas. Nitrogen boils at -196°C. It is used to make fertilizers and nitric acid.
Some liquid oxygen is used to cool the nitrogen and liquefy it. This is possible because the nitrogen is at a higher pressure than the oxygen and so has a higher boiling point.
Argon gas. Argon boils at -186°C and is used as an unreactive filling for some light bulbs.
Liquid oxygen. Oxygen boils at -183°C and is used for breathing apparatus.

Why nitrogen is liquefied under pressure

Chemists make use of the Gas Laws when they are separating nitrogen from other atmospheric gases. These laws describe how a gas behaves and are one of the cornerstones of science.

To make nitrogen into a liquid, where the volume occupied by the molecules is much smaller than a gas, the gas volume has to be reduced.

One of the Gas Laws states:

The volume of a gas reduces as the temperature is *lowered* or if the pressure is *increased*.

This law means that chemists can work with a combination of lowering the temperature and raising the pressure to get the most economical way of liquefying the gas.

Nitrogen

▲ Liquid nitrogen boiling vigorously at room temperature

Uses for inert nitrogen

For many purposes nitrogen can be thought of as an inert gas. This means that it does not react easily with other gases or liquids.

At first this might seem to be a very unpromising property for a gas, but in fact it has found many applications in food packaging, food preservation and light bulbs.

In each case nitrogen is used *because* it doesn't react. For example, nitrogen gas is used in some forms of food processing to prevent oxygen getting to the food and causing it to spoil. Nitrogen gas in light bulbs is designed to make the filaments last much longer.

Preserving food freshness

Food spoils because of the presence of oxygen (which reacts with the food to produce new, less tasty chemical compounds). One way of preserving the freshness of food therefore is to fill the space around the food with nitrogen, which replaces the oxygen and does not react with the food at all. (Sometimes nitrogen is called an antioxidant, i.e., it keeps food from oxidizing.)

Food can be frozen at very low temperatures using nitrogen. During the freezing process the food does not have time to spoil as it would when frozen slowly in air.

Other foods that are prepared by roasting could be severely altered by the presence of oxygen in the air. For example, the flavor of roasting coffee would be lost in air, so coffee is roasted in an oven containing nitrogen.

Some snack food packages are filled with nitrogen for this reason. Look for the inflated foil bags of chips for instance.

◀ The puffed up packaging that is used for some foods is not just to make the food appear to occupy more volume than it really does. The bag contains inert nitrogen, used to prevent the food from spoiling and, in the case of delicate foods like chips, to help to prevent the packaging from being crushed and the chips breaking.

antioxidant: a substance that prevents oxidation of some other substance.

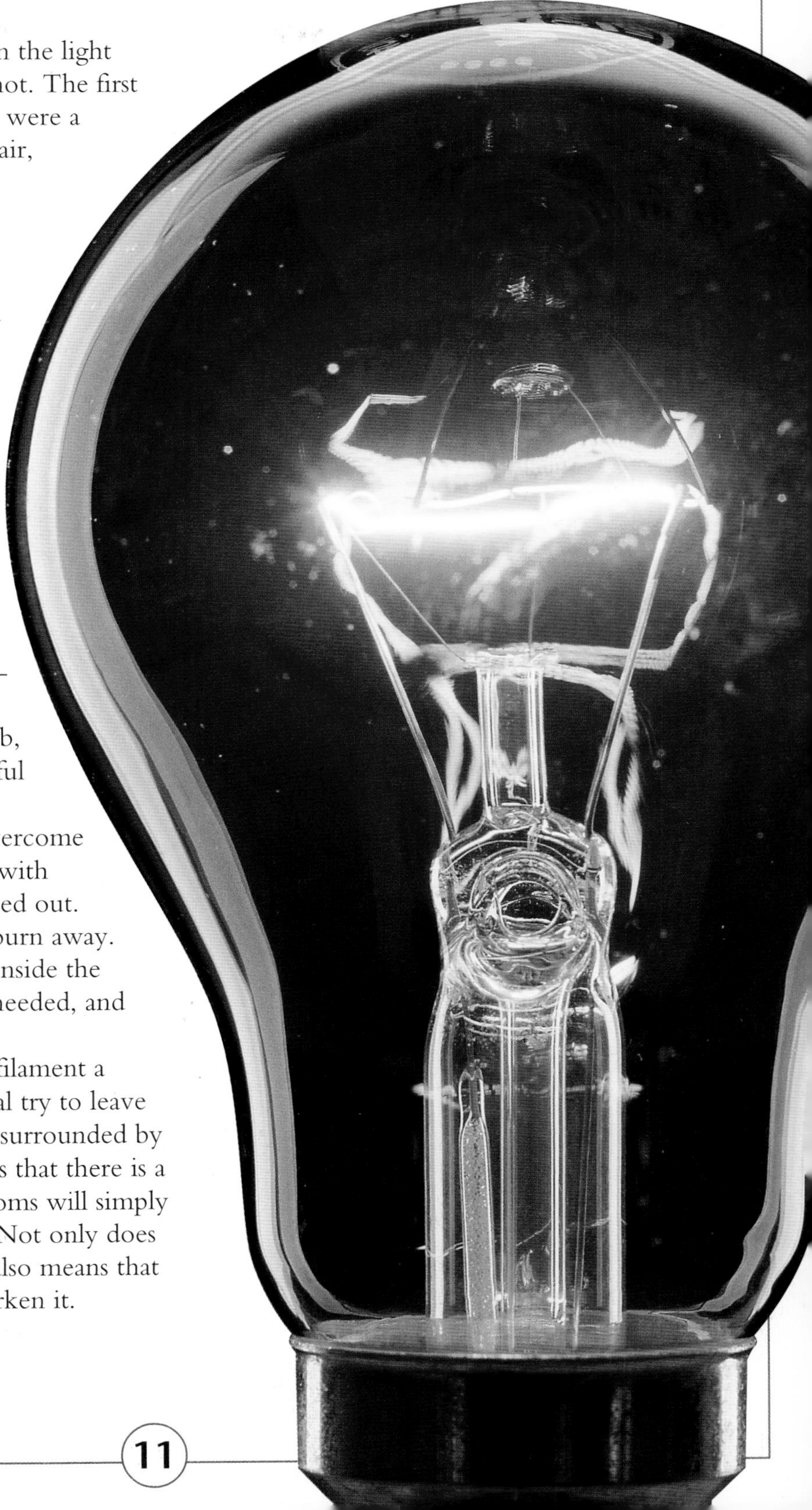

How a light bulb works

Light bulbs (incandescent bulbs) rely on the light given out by a filament as it gets very hot. The first attempts to make an incandescent bulb were a failure because the filament was left in air, where it reacted with the oxygen and burned away within seconds.

To try to solve this problem the filaments were put in a glass bulb from which as much air as possible had been withdrawn. But this was not very successful either. A vacuum is difficult to produce; and if a bulb broke, the resulting implosion of the glass could have caused possible harm to anyone standing nearby. But even if it didn't break, the glass quickly blackened and so became unusable. This is because the hot filament sends out a stream of particles, gradually wasting away (and thus producing a short light-bulb life). Particles of metal were deposited on the inside of the glass bulb, thus darkening it and allowing less useful light to get out.

Both of these disadvantages were overcome using nitrogen gas. By filling the bulb with nitrogen, oxygen is automatically pushed out. This means that the filament will not burn away. At the same time, the presence of gas inside the bulb means that a low pressure is not needed, and the bulb won't implode if it breaks.

The nitrogen also helps to give the filament a longer life. As particles (atoms) of metal try to leave the hot filament, they find themselves surrounded by molecules of nitrogen gas. The result is that there is a much greater chance that the metal atoms will simply bounce back onto the filament again. Not only does this help preserve the filament, but it also means that fewer atoms reach the glass bulb to darken it.

Ammonia

Ammonia, whose formula is NH_3, is a compound of nitrogen and hydrogen. The word may come from an association with the ancient Egyptian god Ammon. In former times ammonia was obtained by boiling animal horns and hoofs.

It is a colorless gas that is not actually poisonous; but inhaling its fumes can cause people to stop breathing, so it can have very serious effects.

Ammonia can always be detected by its irritating smell. It is famous for its use as "smelling salts" in the last century, in which a compound of ammonia, ammonium carbonate, was used. Smelling salts were used to revive women who had swooned (not actually fainted, but who were putting on a show as a social gesture that they had been offended). It was very difficult to continue to pretend to have fainted when the smell of ammonia was irritating the throat, and so they "revived."

Ammonia is extremely soluble in water, where it produces an alkaline liquid, ammonium hydroxide. This dilute solution is commonly sold for use in household disinfectants and cleaning under the title household ammonia.

Ammonia is also one of the most important starting materials for making artificial fertilizers.

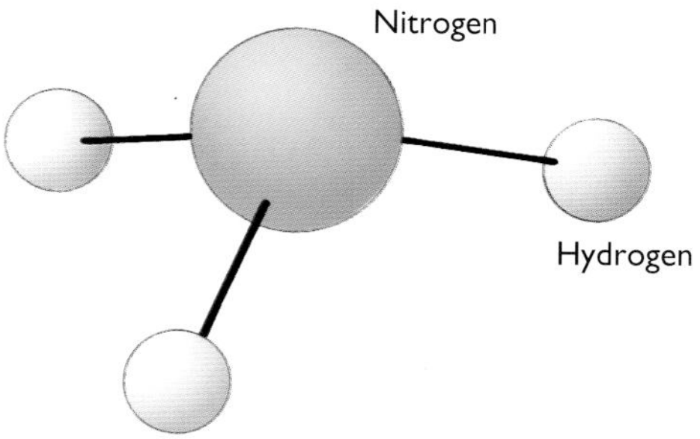

▲ A representation of an ammonia molecule.

Ammonia for refrigeration

Ammonia gas has a high boiling point (about -33°C). It also absorbs a large amount of heat energy as it vaporizes. It is not corrosive and is easy to obtain. This makes it particularly suitable for use in refrigeration systems, which work by boiling and then liquefying a material as it passes through the refrigeration pipework.

► Ammonia can be added to irrigation water and applied to fields at the same time as they are watered. In such diluted amounts its smell cannot be detected.

alkaline: the opposite of acidic. Alkalis are bases that dissolve, and alkaline materials are called basic materials. Solutions of alkalis have a pH greater than 7.0 because they contain relatively few hydrogen ions.

resin: resins are natural or synthetic polymers. They can be molded into solid objects or spun into thread.

soluble: a substance that will readily dissolve in a solvent.

◀ The TransAlaskan pipeline uses refrigeration by ammonia in the thousands of legs that support the pipeline over permafrost areas. The refrigerated legs are needed to prevent the permafrost from melting, allowing the legs to founder and causing the pipeline to fracture.

▶ A representation of a urea molecule.

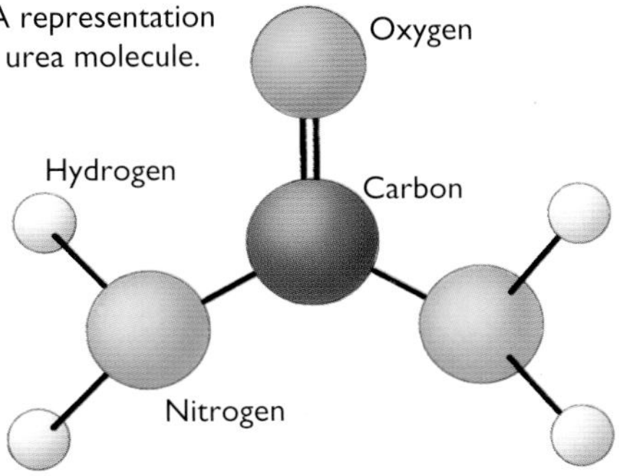
Oxygen
Hydrogen
Carbon
Nitrogen

Uses of ammonia

About three-quarters of the ammonia produced is used to make fertilizers. It can be sprayed on crops, on the ground or injected as a gas into the soil. Because it is so soluble it can also be readily added to irrigation water.

Ammonia is also a starting material for a substance called urea, $CO(NH_2)_2$, which is used as a fertilizer in its own right and also in the manufacture of resins, some cosmetics and medicines.

If ammonia is not used directly as a fertilizer, it is mainly converted to ammonium nitrate by reacting ammonia with nitric acid. Ammonium nitrate can also be used in explosives such as TNT and dynamite (see page 27).

Ammonium chloride is used as a cleaning agent for metals prior to their being painted, galvanized or soldered. Ammonium chloride is also found in the paste inside all zinc-carbon dry cell batteries.

Ammonia is also used by some craftspeople because, when soaked into wood, it makes the wood behave as a plastic that can then be shaped. As the ammonia evaporates, the wood again becomes hard.

EQUATION: Reaction of ammonia and nitric acid

Ammonia + nitric acid ⇨ ammonium nitrate

$NH_3(aq) + HNO_3(aq) \Rightarrow NH_4NO_3(aq)$

Soluble alkaline ammonia

Ammonia is an alkaline substance, so it will cause a color change in a chemical indicator. Ammonia is also extremely soluble, and one volume of water will dissolve four hundred times its own volume of ammonia. The density of the solution falls to 0.880 grams per milliliter as it becomes saturated, and the solution is known as "880 ammonia."

Both of these properties of ammonia can be demonstrated in a dramatic way, in a classic laboratory experiment shown on this page.

Preparing dry ammonia in the laboratory

Ammonium sulfate and calcium hydroxide are ground up and mixed using a pestle and mortar. The mixture is put into a long-necked, round-bottomed flask, and the neck clamped so that it points downward.

The mixture is heated. The heat energy causes a reaction, and ammonia and water vapor are given off. The (wet) ammonia gas is passed through a vertical column (called a drying tower) containing calcium oxide (another base, so no reaction occurs). The calcium oxide (lime) takes up the water from the ammonia (to make calcium hydroxide, slaked lime), and the dry ammonia gas now passes to an inverted collecting flask. Here it displaces air from the flask because ammonia has a lower density than air.

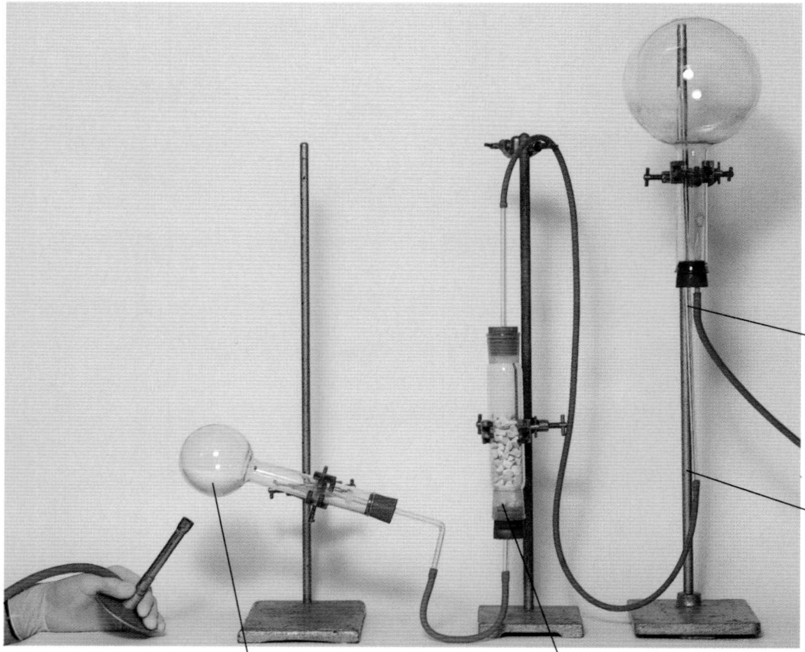

◀ Laboratory apparatus for preparing dry ammonia.

EQUATION: Producing ammonia in the laboratory

Ammonium sulfate + calcium hydroxide ⇨ ammonia + water + calcium sulfate

$$(NH_4)_2SO_4(s) + Ca(OH)_2(s) \Rightarrow 2NH_3(g) + 2H_2O(l) + CaSO_4(s)$$

An ammonia fountain

❶ The preparation apparatus is removed, the short exit tube is blocked and the long entry tube is led from the flask to a trough of water containing a chemical indicator. The indicator is colorless because the water is neutral.

❷ Ether liquid is poured onto the flask, causing the temperature of the gas to drop. The gas therefore contracts, and the pressure inside the flask is reduced.

Air pressure is now able to push water from the trough up the thin tube and into the flask.

As soon as the first drops of water come into contact with the ammonia gas, the ammonia goes into solution and there is a rapid drop of pressure in the flask. Air pressure then causes the water to spurt into the flask, producing the fountain.

❸ and ❹ The flask fills with bright red water as the ammonia turns the water alkaline and the chemical indicator (phenolphthalein) turns red.

alkaline: the opposite of acidic. Alkalis are bases that dissolve, and alkaline materials are called basic materials. Solutions of alkalis have a pH greater than 7.0 because they contain relatively few hydrogen ions.

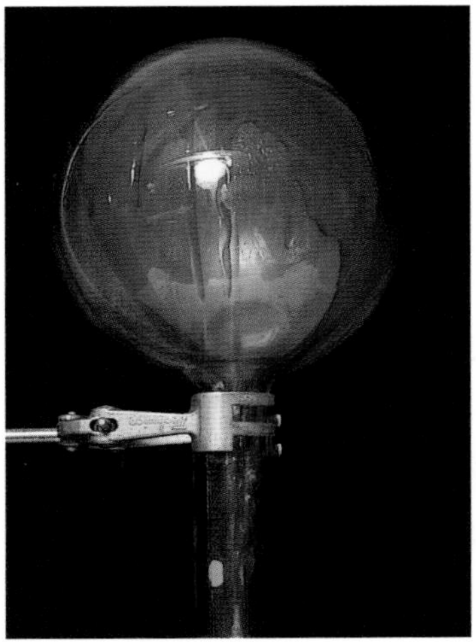

▲❷ The ammonia fountain begins.

▼❶ The apparatus before the ammonia fountain.

▼►❸ and ❹ The red color of the liquid is the effect of the indicator showing the presence of an alkaline solution.

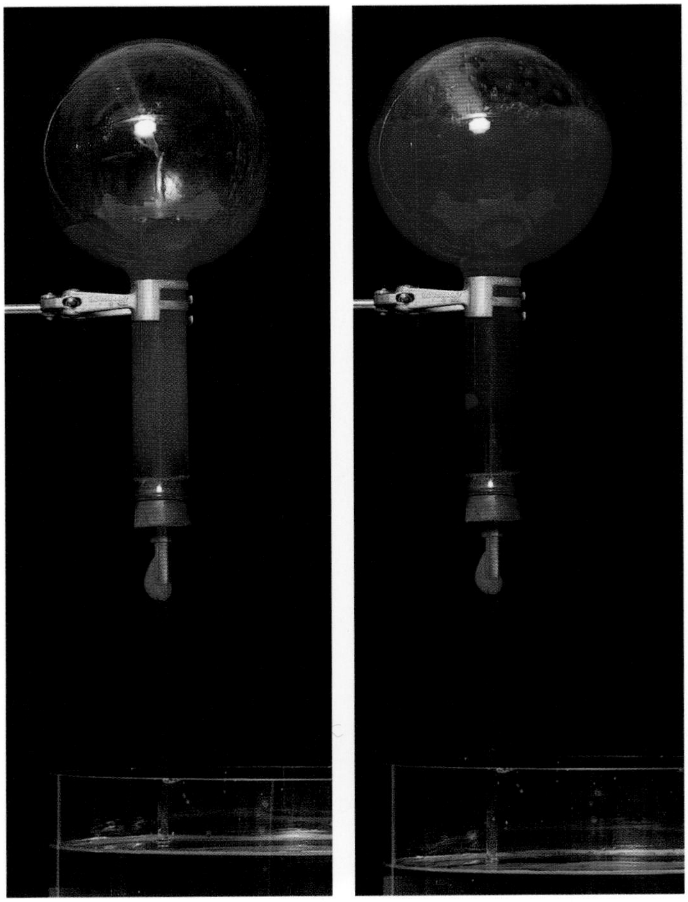

Making ammonia industrially

The industrial method of making ammonia is called the Haber-Bosch process after its inventors. In the process, nitrogen and hydrogen gases are reacted at high temperatures (up to 600°C) and high pressures (up to 600 atmospheres). The reaction works best if this is done in the presence of iron, although iron is a catalyst in the reaction and so remains unchanged.

The ammonia produced is liquefied to separate it from the unreacted gases, which are then recycled.

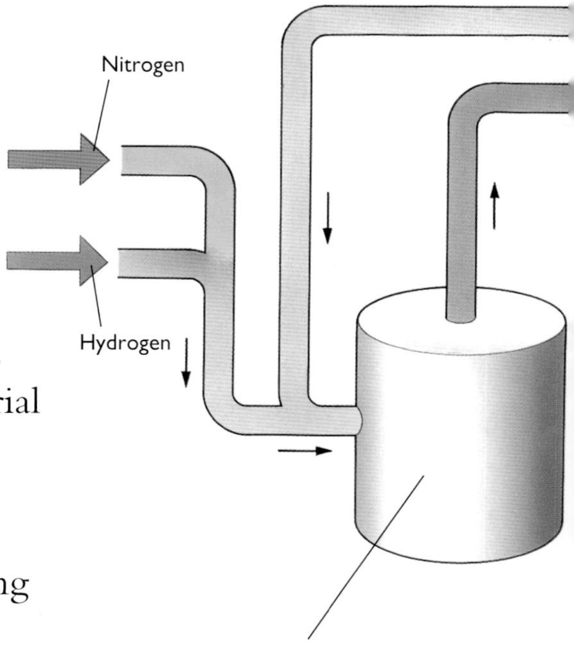

The mixture of gases is put under great pressure and heated to a high temperature.

Limitations of the Haber-Bosch process

This process has produced the foundation material for important fertilizers and has thus greatly contributed to the increase in the world's food supply. However, the process consumes large amounts of energy; and the equipment, operating at high temperatures and pressures, is expensive to make.

The source of hydrogen from the reaction is mainly petroleum, a nonrenewable fossil fuel. For this reason, fertilizers are expensive and scientists are looking for a natural way to fix nitrogen for use as a fertilizer.

EQUATION: Production of ammonia by the Haber-Bosch process

Hydrogen+ nitrogen ⇨ ammonia

$3H_2(g) + N_2(g) \Rightarrow 2NH_3(g)$

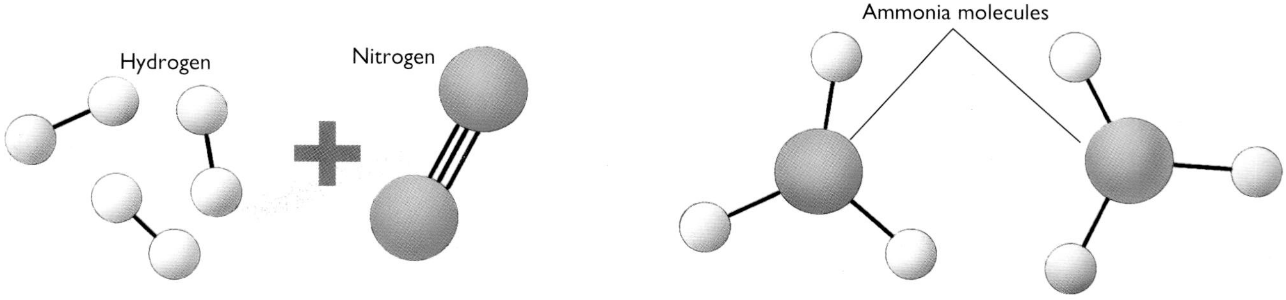

In the main chamber nitrogen and hydrogen are passed over finely divided iron, which acts as a catalyst. The tower is designed to provide a very large surface area on which the gases can react in the presence of the catalyst. In this chamber much of the hydrogen and nitrogen is converted to ammonia.

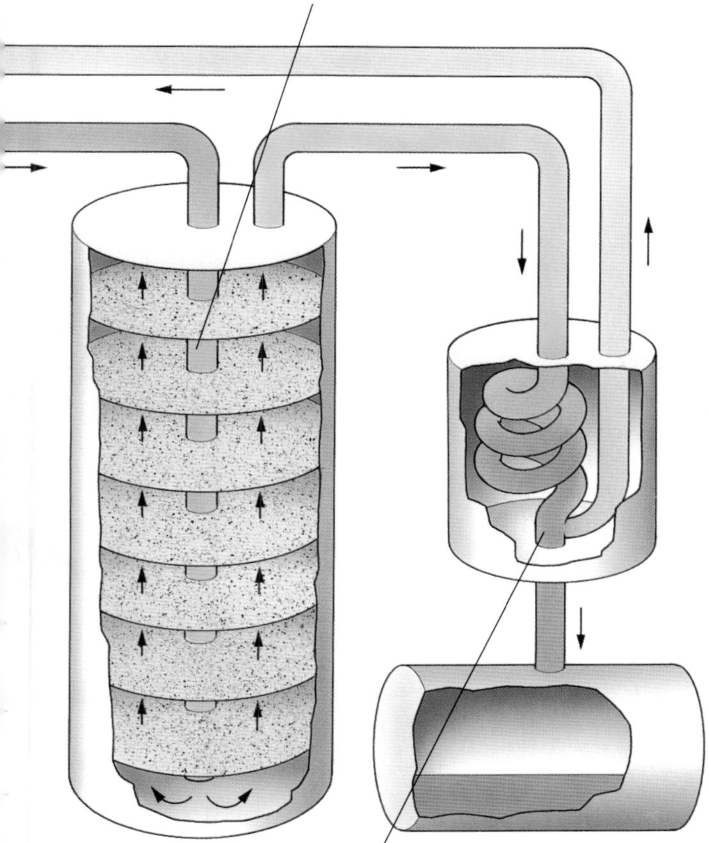

The gases are cooled, and ammonia is liquefied and drawn off the base of the cooling chamber. The unreacted gases are recycled back to the catalytic chamber.

catalyst: a substance that speeds up a chemical reaction but itself remains unaltered at the end of the reaction.

fixing: a term applied especially to nitrogen to describe the way that the gas nitrogen can be made into solid and liquid nitrogen-containing compounds that can be used as fertilizers.

Also... Ammonia as a source of hydrogen

Hydrogen is a highly inflammable gas that is dangerous to transport. To solve this problem, hydrogen is often transported in the form of safe liquid ammonia. When it reaches its destination, the ammonia is heated and decomposes to one-quarter nitrogen and three-quarters hydrogen.

◄▲ The catalytic towers in an ammonia plant.

Naturally fixed nitrogen

Nitrogen can be made in a chemical plant for use as a fertilizer. However, there are natural processes that perform a much more efficient job of "fixing" nitrogen into a form that is available for plant use.

Several species of bacteria, fungi and blue-green algae are able to "fix" nitrogen. They convert nitrogen into ammonia, a soluble material that can be absorbed by plants.

One of the most common nitrogen-fixing group of bacteria is called *Rhizobium*. These bacteria make the nodules, or galls, on the roots of legumes (plants like clover, beans, peanuts and alfalfa).

Both the bacteria and the plants benefit from this relationship. The bacteria need the plants for food; the waste products of the bacteria are nitrogen compounds, which are important to plant growth.

Natural nitrogen-producers are an efficient method of applying nitrogen fertilizer to a field. This is why, for several centuries, legumes have been grown alternately (in rotation) with "nitrogen-hungry" crops like wheat and barley.

Nitrogen-fixing bacteria can also be used to improve the yields of water-loving plants such as rice. In the flooded rice-paddy fields the nitrogen is fixed by blue-green algae that live together with species of water fern. By planting this fern in rice fields, nitrogen compounds are fixed and released into the water where they can be absorbed by the roots of rice plants.

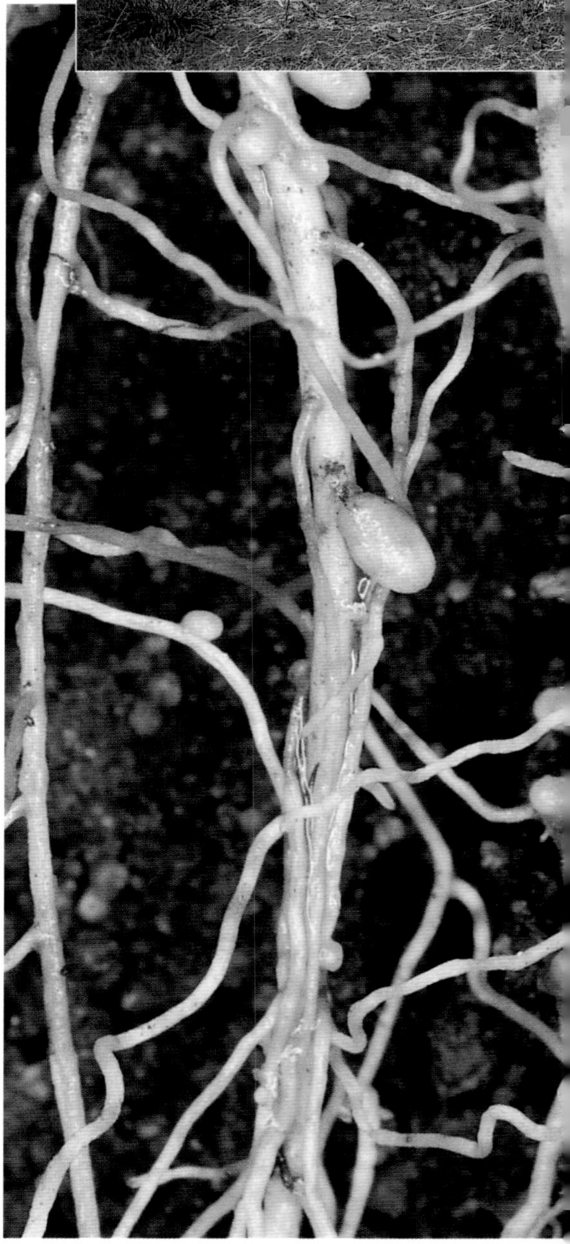

◀ A wide range of leguminous plants, for example, these tropical acacias, exist in the world.

▶ Blue-green algae in the water that floods a paddy field are able to fix nitrogen.

▼ Nodules on a nitrogen-fixing legume.

fixing: a term applied especially to nitrogen to describe the way that the gas nitrogen can be made into solid and liquid nitrogen-containing compounds that can be used as fertilizers.

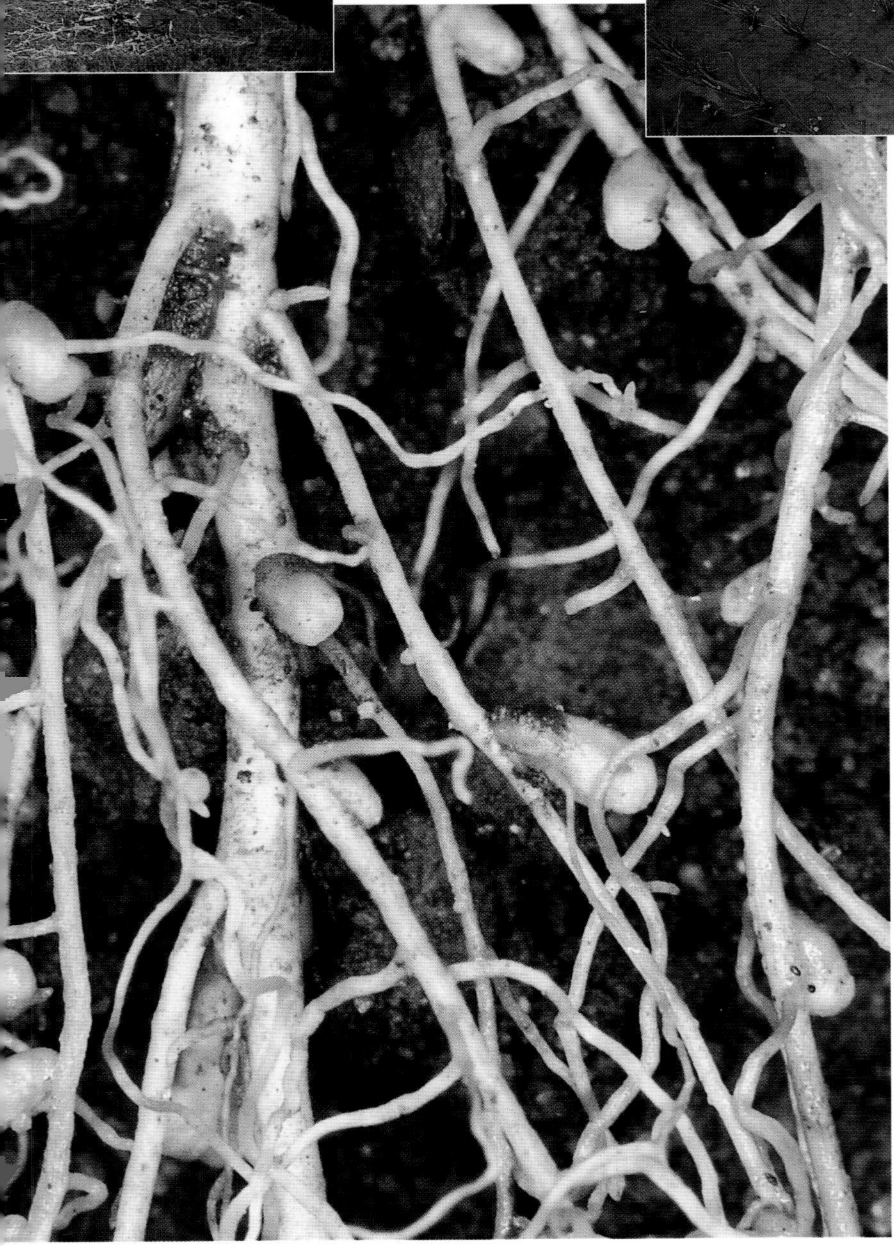

The importance of natural sources of fixed nitrogen

About one kilogram of nitrogen may be fixed (made into nitrogen-containing compounds) per hectare of the Earth's surface per year by lightning flashes.

However, the majority of nitrogen is fixed in the soil. Bacteria in legume nodules extract about fifty kilograms of nitrogen per hectare from soil air, while other forms of bacteria not connected to legumes fix a further five kilograms per hectare per year.

Yet despite these seemingly large amounts of nitrogen fixed from the air, they only make up about one-third of the total requirements of growing plants, and the remainder must come from recycling nitrogen as compost and manure or from artificial supplies.

Nitrogen-based fertilizers

Plants obtain their nitrogen as soluble nitrate compounds. Nitrogen-based fertilizers (in the form of soluble nitrate) are among the most important of all aids to producing more crops for the world to eat.

Using manure is the natural ("organic") way of applying nitrogen fertilizer in addition to that in rainfall or produced by legumes and soil bacteria. Using manure is a way of recycling waste products, and an added advantage is that manure contains a wide variety of elements in addition to nitrogen that can be used for the benefit of plants and the soil.

Manure tends to act slowly, relying on bacteria to break down the waste organic matter. As part of the process of breakdown, bacteria release nitrogen as ammonia and soluble nitrates.

For more immediate, as well as sometimes more convenient, application, concentrated nitrogen-containing fertilizers obtained from nitrate rock or produced from ammonia are applied to a soil.

Applying nitrate fertilizer

There are several methods of applying nitrogen fertilizer. On highly mechanized farms it may be applied in the form of an ammonia solution in water that is injected about 15 cm under the soil's surface to prevent the liquid from vaporizing. More commonly, a solution containing ammonia compounds is sprayed onto the fields.

To make the number of applications less frequent, fertilizer can be applied in pellet form. The pellets dissolve and release nitrates throughout a growing season.

Artificial fertilizers do have limitations, however, and not just because they may pollute rivers and lakes. The rapid growth that can occur with some very concentrated formulations can cause the crop to have less taste, be "watery" and have other less desirable qualities. For these reasons, research continues into how to make more effective use of natural nitrogen fixation, producing genetic engineering that may allow all plants in the future to fix their own nitrogen.

► A stick containing nitrate pushed into the soil of a house-plant.

▲ Potassium nitrate occurs naturally as the mineral niter, which is found in abundance in Chile and in much smaller deposits as a white crust in rocks and caves.

Nitrate-containing rocks

Rocks containing nitrogen are uncommon. They consist mainly of a rock called saltpeter (potassium nitrate), the largest source of which is in the deserts of Chile. Because natural supplies of nitrates are so scarce and the need for fertilizers so important, countries are reluctant to be dependent on such overseas sources. As a result, the Haber-Bosch process of using ammonia (see page 16) has been adopted throughout the world.

▶ The majority of ammonium nitrate is produced from ammonia using the Haber-Bosch process.

Nitrogen cycle

Nitrogen is continually transferred between the land, animals, plants and the atmosphere in a never-ending cycle. This nitrogen cycle is one of the most important cycles for life on Earth. Its main stages are summarized here from the detail provided on the previous pages:

❶ The cycle begins when lightning flashes provide the energy for atmospheric nitrogen and oxygen to combine to form dilute nitric acid.

❷ Several species of bacteria, fungi and blue-green algae can convert nitrogen into nitrogen-containing compounds such as nitrates. These compounds are then used in photosynthesis to make new sources of energy for the growth of plant tissue.

❸ Along the food chain, animals use the nitrogen locked up in plant and animal tissues as a way of getting the nitrogen they need to build new cells. The nitrogen is obtained during the process of digestion.

❹ All animals produce waste nitrogen in the form of a nitrogen-containing compound called urea. This is removed from the body during excretion. It will either evaporate or be broken down by bacteria. Nitrogen-containing compounds are very soluble, and rainwater may wash them into rivers, where they may cause pollution problems.

❺ Bacteria involved in decomposing waste and dead material release nitrogen from its compounds, forming gas that can escape to the atmosphere, thus completing the cycle.

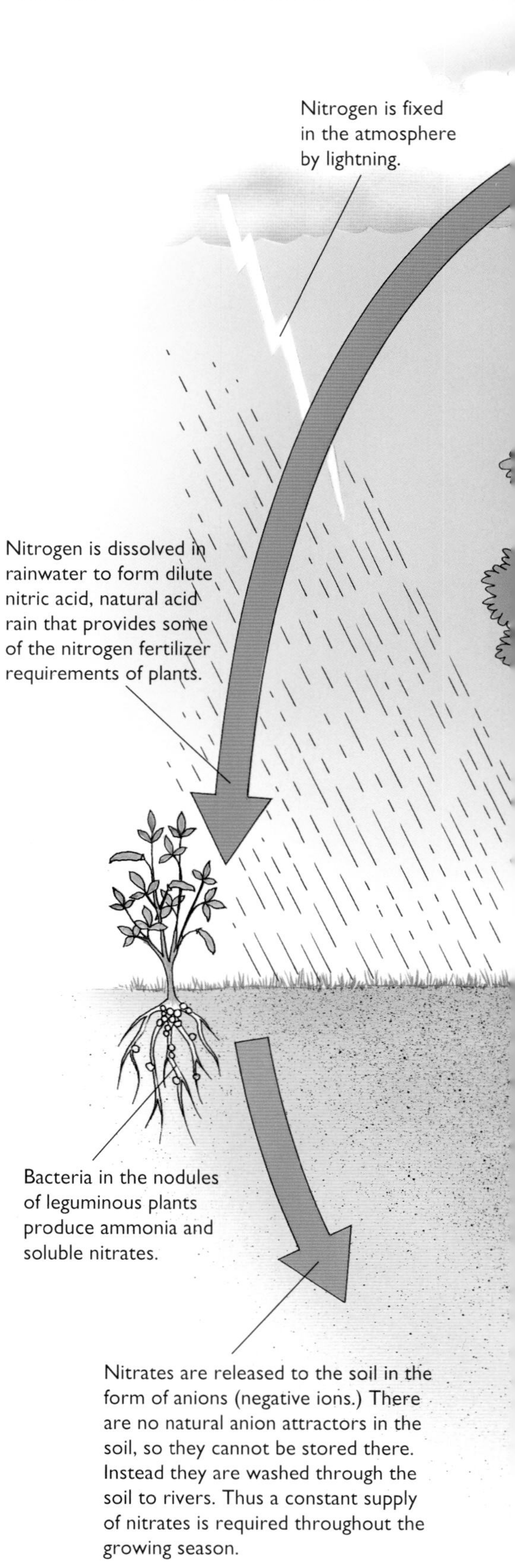

Nitrogen is fixed in the atmosphere by lightning.
Nitrogen is dissolved in rainwater to form dilute nitric acid, natural acid rain that provides some of the nitrogen fertilizer requirements of plants.
Bacteria in the nodules of leguminous plants produce ammonia and soluble nitrates.
Nitrates are released to the soil in the form of anions (negative ions.) There are no natural anion attractors in the soil, so they cannot be stored there. Instead they are washed through the soil to rivers. Thus a constant supply of nitrates is required throughout the growing season.

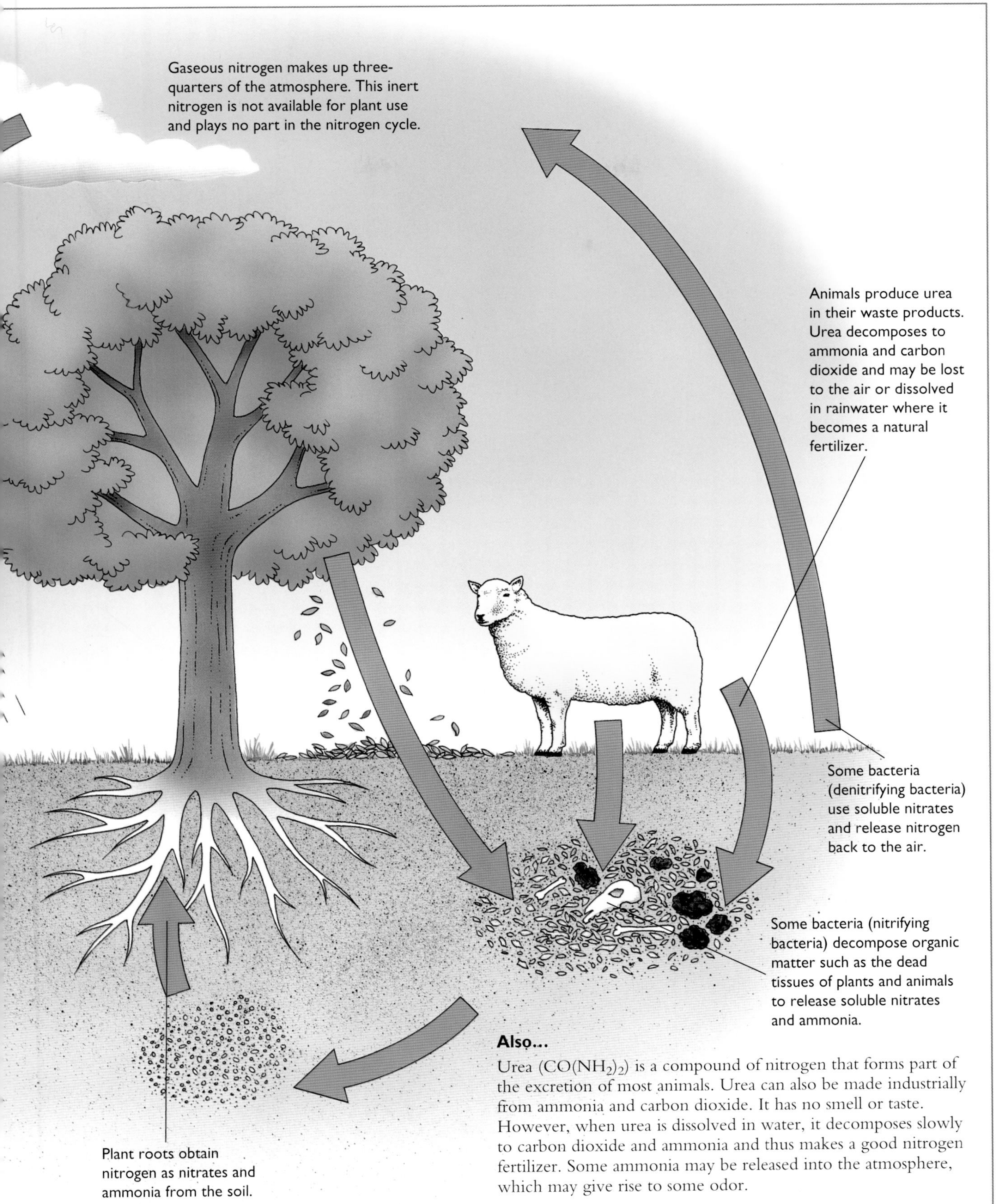
Gaseous nitrogen makes up three-quarters of the atmosphere. This inert nitrogen is not available for plant use and plays no part in the nitrogen cycle.
Animals produce urea in their waste products. Urea decomposes to ammonia and carbon dioxide and may be lost to the air or dissolved in rainwater where it becomes a natural fertilizer.
Some bacteria (denitrifying bacteria) use soluble nitrates and release nitrogen back to the air.
Some bacteria (nitrifying bacteria) decompose organic matter such as the dead tissues of plants and animals to release soluble nitrates and ammonia.
Plant roots obtain nitrogen as nitrates and ammonia from the soil.

Also...

Urea ($CO(NH_2)_2$) is a compound of nitrogen that forms part of the excretion of most animals. Urea can also be made industrially from ammonia and carbon dioxide. It has no smell or taste. However, when urea is dissolved in water, it decomposes slowly to carbon dioxide and ammonia and thus makes a good nitrogen fertilizer. Some ammonia may be released into the atmosphere, which may give rise to some odor.

Demonstrating nitrogen-based explosives

Solids and liquids occupy very little volume compared with the same number of molecules of a compound as a gas. The rapid change from solid or liquid to gas is the key to creating an explosion.

An explosive is a substance that is normally unreactive but which can be made to react very violently, changing from a solid or a liquid to a gas. The explosion is created because of the pressure of the expanding gas on surrounding solid or liquid materials.

Many explosive materials simply burn when they are not contained in some form of packing. Thus, for example, gunpowder can be laid as a trail of powder to make a burning fuse; but if the trail leads to gunpowder confined in a barrel, the gunpowder will explode. This shows that the process of burning is quite slow, and that a container is needed so that pressure can build up to give an explosive effect.

Many materials can be made explosive. For example, gas vapors can explode, as can coal dust and even flour dust. Thus, providing a material with a large amount of surface area – as happens with powders – also helps to create an explosion.

▼ The relative space occupied by a solid, liquid and a gas helps us to understand the effect of explosives. A sudden change of state of a substance from a solid to a gas creates a rapid expansion and consequent displacement of whatever material is around that substance.

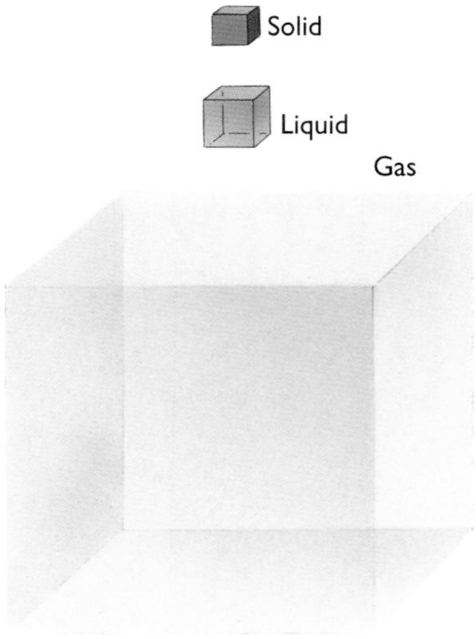

▶ Orange ammonium dichromate crystals are dense and occupy relatively little space. During the reaction shown, nitrogen is released as a gas, leaving green chromium oxide behind.

Boiling tube cannon

In the demonstration on this page some crystals of orange ammonium dichromate have been strongly heated in a boiling tube. This adds heat energy to the crystals. Notice that the boiling tube is heated at the open end. This means that the reaction first occurs in the crystals near the open end, and only later in those near the closed end.

The first change is that the crystals glow red hot. At this point, the external heating is removed. The chemical decomposition gives out heat (as nitrogen molecules form), which causes the reaction to spread along the mixture. The crystals decompose to give nitrogen gas, water (as steam) and a bulky green solid called chromium oxide.

As the reaction continues, the chromium oxide blocks the open end of the tube, so as the heat energy is used to create nitrogen gas, pressure builds up toward the closed end of the tube until eventually the gas pressure is enough to shoot the chromium oxide out as fragments. This explosive violence is similar to the way ash is shot out from a volcano, or cannonballs, grapeshot or shells fly out of a piece of artillery. In every case it is the rapid creation of nitrogen gas that builds up pressure and eventually breaks apart any nearby solids.

decompose: to break down a substance (for example, by heat or with the aid of a catalyst) into simpler components. In such a chemical reaction only one substance is involved.

explosive: a substance which, when a shock is applied to it, decomposes very rapidly, releasing a very large amount of heat and creating a large volume of gases as a shock wave.

▼ Fine particles of chromium oxide are ejected from the boiling tube cannon.

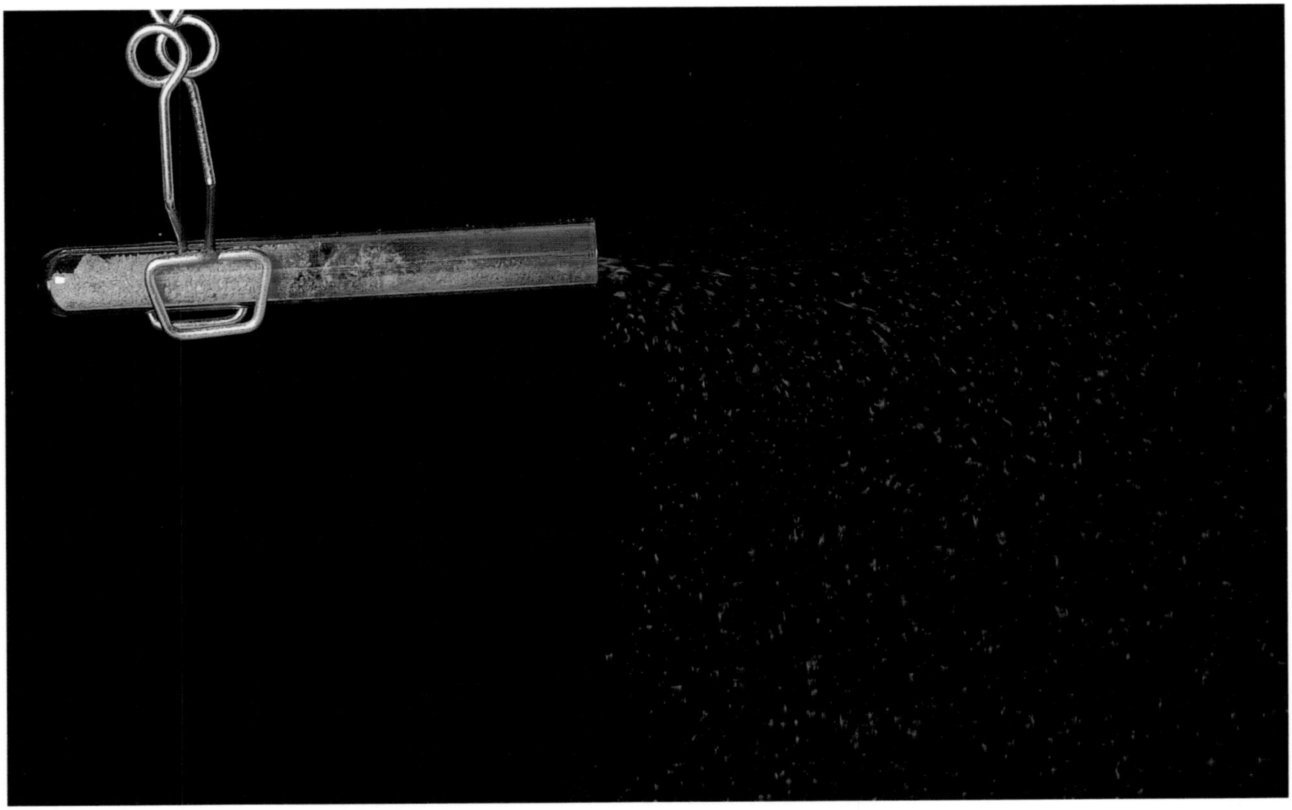

EQUATION: Heating ammonium dichromate

Ammonium dichromate ➪ nitrogen + chromium oxide + water

$(NH_4)_2Cr_2O_7(s)$ ➪ $N_2(g)$ + $Cr_2O_3(s)$ + $4H_2O(l)$

Nitrogen-containing explosives

Explosives design is a very specialized form of chemistry. Explosives can be used for propelling bullets and shells for use in war, but they can also be used for a wide range of peaceful purposes. Each type of explosive has its own exploding characteristics, described here.

▲ By 1242 Roger Bacon was using a mixture of 41.2 parts saltpeter, 29.4 parts charcoal, and 29.4 parts sulfur for his gunpowder in making fireworks. A gunpowder mixture is still used for fireworks, such as this catherine wheel.

Gunpowder

The world's first true explosive, gunpowder, was invented in China in about 1000 AD. It is a mixture of 10% sulfur, 15% charcoal, and 75% potassium nitrate.

Gunpowder is one of the most important chemicals ever to be invented, because by allowing people to use explosive devices, including guns and cannons, it changed the course of history.

Gunpowder was particularly easy to make explode because it is very sensitive to sparks. However, this same property meant that accidents were common. To reduce the chances of accidental explosions, gunpowder was mixed with graphite.

The main uses for gunpowder today are for fireworks, in artillery shells and fuses for hand grenades.

▼ Many guns use explosives derived from nitrogen.

Nitroglycerin and dynamite

Glyceryl trinitrate (called nitroglycerin) is the most unstable of the common explosives. It is a pale yellow oil prepared by reacting nitric acid with glycerol (a product of oil refineries).

Alfred Nobel was the first to make a stable form of nitroglycerin by making it into a solid. In this way he created the world's most widely used high explosive – dynamite.

explosive: a substance which, when a shock is applied to it, decomposes very rapidly, releasing a very large amount of heat and creating a large volume of gases as a shock wave.

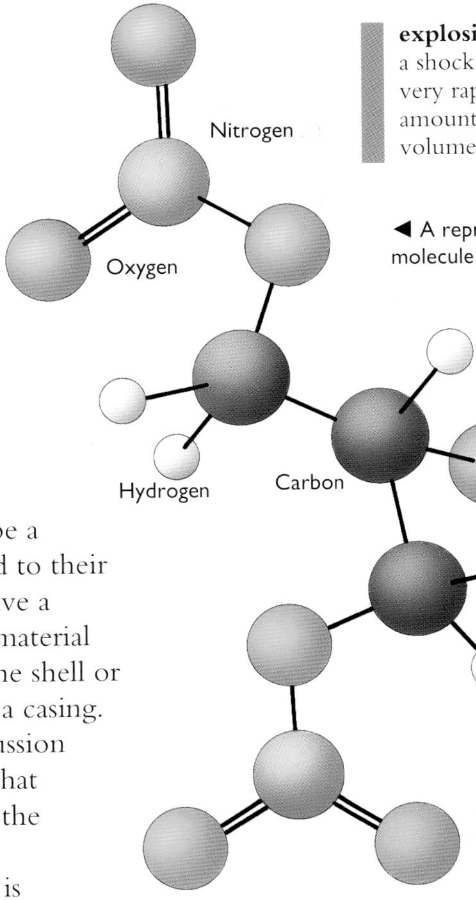
Nitrogen
Oxygen
Hydrogen
Carbon

◀ A representation of a molecule of nitroglycerine

Ammunition

Ammunition is the word used to describe a wide variety of objects that are propelled to their target. Any piece of ammunition will have a primer, or detonator, a propellant, the material that explodes, and a projectile, such as the shell or bullet. All of this is usually contained in a casing.

Most modern primers are called percussion caps. They contain sensitive explosives that detonate on a shock from, for example, the hammer of a gun.

The main propellant for ammunition is nitrocellulose. This was traditionally called guncotton, because at one time cotton fibers were soaked in liquid explosive. Modern guncotton uses wood fiber.

Projectiles used to be small lead balls. Modern ammunition is clad in brass or copper and is given a more streamlined shape that we recognize as bullets.

▲ Connecting the detonator to an explosive charge.

TNT

TNT is the abbreviation for trinitrotoluene, the most common high explosive. It is produced by reacting toluene with nitric acid in the presence of sulfuric acid.

The advantage of TNT is that it is not sensitive to shocks and so can be handled without risk of accidental explosion. It can even be burned without exploding.

TNT has a low melting point (about 80°C), so it can be melted with steam and poured into the casings of gun shells.

Detonators

Most high explosives can only be detonated with the shock from another explosive. This is why most explosive devices have a main explosive and a detonator. The detonator, or blasting cap, contains small amounts of more sensitive explosive to set off a larger reaction.

There are several common detonating explosives, such as PETN (pentaerythrite tetranitrate), used in blasting caps. RDX (cyclotrimethylenetrinitramine) produces the highest energy yield and detonation pressure of any common explosive. Mixtures of RDX with plastic materials make "plastic explosive." Ammonium nitrate explodes with a blast that is less violent and sudden than many other explosions. This is used to move an obstacle rather than to shatter it. Amatol (ammonium nitrite and TNT) is used as a blasting charge.

Peaceful explosions

People often associate explosives with death and wanton destruction. However, the vast majority of explosives are used for peaceful purposes, such as to blast rock from quarries or to demolish buildings without damaging the surrounding area.

All explosives decompose to release both gas and heat. It is often thought that because of this, explosives cause fires. However, explosives are often used to put out fires, such as when burning oil wells have to be capped. Here the expanding nitrogen gas deprives the burning oil of the oxygen it needs to keep burning, and so the flame goes out. At the same time, any hot material is thrown clear so it cannot reignite the oil. The oil will then continue to gush but will not relight.

Explosives used for demolition

Different explosives are suited to different types of building. RDX (see page 27) is the main explosive used for demolishing skyscrapers with steel frames. Dynamite is used to demolish reinforced concrete buildings.

Most demolition experts use relatively small charges placed in holes drilled into the structure. Demolition aims to achieve a progressive collapse of the structure so that it falls in on itself without creating too much dust.

▼ A large road bridge is demolished using explosives.

▲ Modern air bags are filled with sodium azide.

Azide: explosive air bags of nitrogen

No gas cylinder lies behind the life-saving air bag. Everything happens in a flash because of nitrogen chemistry. Nitrogen is produced within one-thousandth of a second, far faster than a gas cylinder could release a supply. Nitrogen is also inert, so it will not contribute to a fire.

Sodium azide is a compound of sodium and nitrogen. All azides are shock sensitive, and lead azide is used as a detonator in some explosives.

Sodium azide is used in air bags, where it is detonated by an electrical device that is itself triggered by sudden deceleration. Sodium azide decomposes very quickly, releasing nitrogen gas that inflates the air bag.

◀ The hundreds of oil-well fires started deliberately by the retreating Iraqi troops during the Gulf War needed to be extinguished quickly because of the environmental damage that was being created. Most were snuffed out using explosives.

Nitrogen dioxide

The three most important gases of nitrogen are nitrogen dioxide (a brown gas that is the cause of the brown part of modern smog) and nitrous and nitric oxides (both colorless gases). All three gases are present in the emissions from vehicles and contribute in various ways to acid rain.

The properties of nitrogen dioxide can be investigated by preparing it in a gas jar in the laboratory or as shown on page 32. Its effects on the environment are discussed on page 34.

❶► Nitrogen dioxide is prepared by pouring concentrated nitric acid onto copper shavings.

❷► As the gas forms, it is a strong brown color. When it has filled the gas jar, it spills over the sides and sinks down the outside of the jar, creating a sinister brown layer on the bench top.

▼ A representation of a molecule of nitrogen dioxide gas.

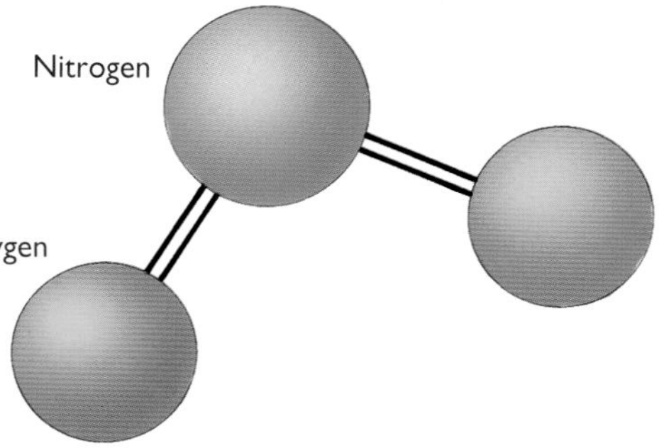

EQUATION: Copper and nitric acid

Copper + nitric acid ➪ copper nitrate + water + nitrogen dioxide

$$Cu(s) + 4HNO_3(conc) \Rightarrow Cu(NO_3)_2(aq) + 2H_2O(l) + 2NO_2(g)$$

Also...

Copper is not very reactive, but it will react with concentrated nitric acid, which acts as an oxidizing agent rather than an acid.

acid rain: rain that is contaminated by acid gases such as sulfur dioxide and nitrogen oxides released by pollution.

oxidizing agent: a substance that removes electrons from another substance (and therefore is itself reduced).

smog: a mixture of smoke and fog. The term is used to describe city fogs in which there is a large proportion of particulate matter (tiny pieces of carbon from exhausts) and also a high concentration of sulfur and nitrogen gases and probably ozone.

❸▼ At the end of the demonstration, water is added to give a blue copper nitrate solution. Nitrogen dioxide is very soluble in water, so the gas jar rapidly clears of the brown gas.

Nitrogen dioxide dissolved in water is nitric acid, one of the two main components of acid rain.

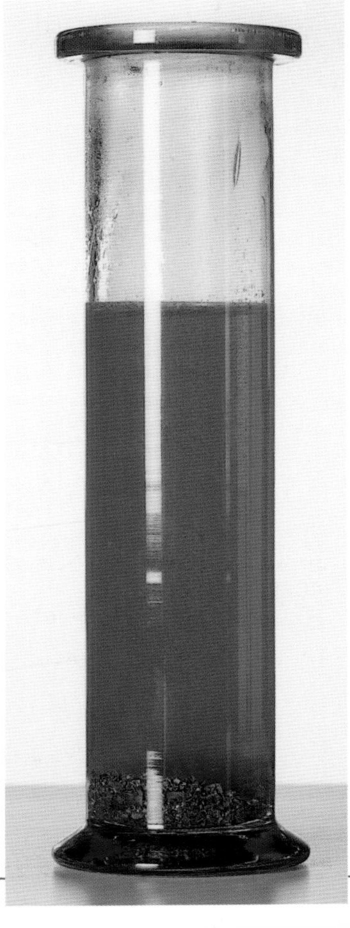

Preparing nitrogen dioxide

This demonstration shows how nitrogen dioxide is produced and what happens if it is cooled.

The demonstration uses lead nitrate as a source of gases. Lead is not a very reactive metal. As a result, its compounds are not very stable and they decompose easily. This is why lead nitrate is a good substance to use for a laboratory demonstration.

In this demonstration lead nitrate is heated. Heating causes the lead nitrate to decompose to lead oxide. During this process energy is released, which can be heard as the crystals of lead nitrate break up.

This breaking down process is called decrepitation. It releases both nitrogen oxides and oxygen, as shown by the gas collected at the end of the apparatus.

In the final stage the gases are dissolved in water, creating nitric acid. In the atmosphere nitrogen dioxide would dissolve in raindrops, helping give rise to a natural fertilizer or, in greater concentrations, to acid rain.

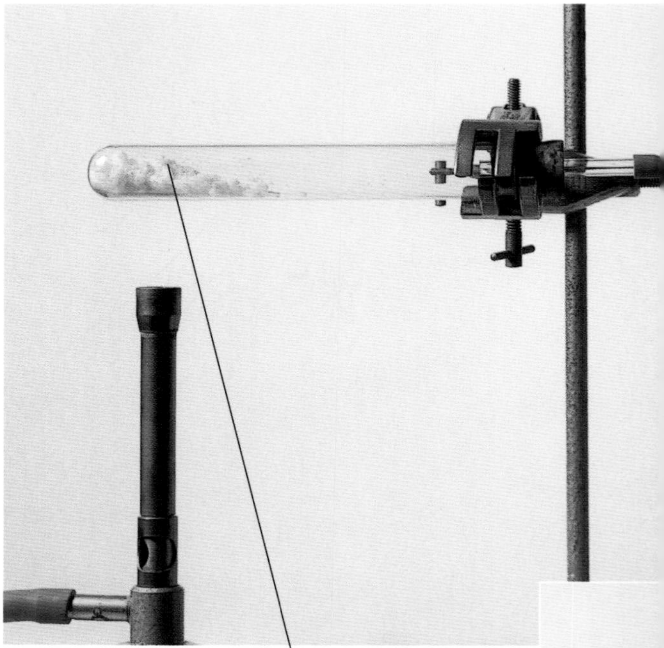

❶ Lead nitrate, a white powder, is heated. It changes color as it melts and decomposes to lead oxide. The bubbles and the brown fumes are oxygen gas and nitrogen oxides, which will be separated out in step 2.

The U-tube for condensing the gas is partly immersed in an ice bath during the experiment.

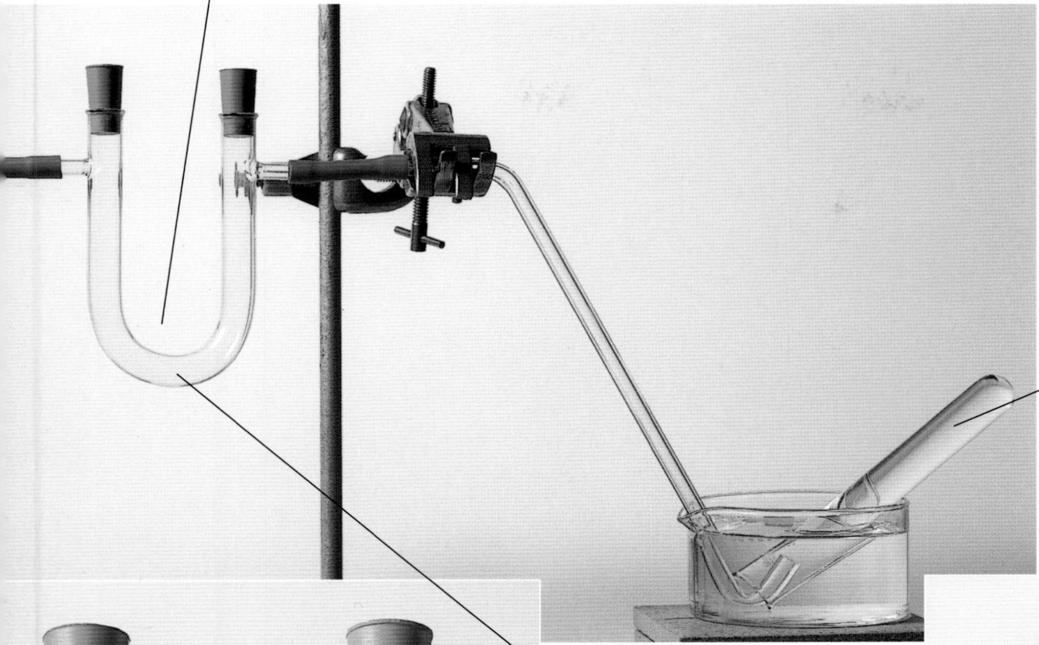

❹ Any nitrogen dioxide not collected in the U-tube dissolves in water to produce nitric acid. Oxygen gas (which, in contrast to nitrogen gases, is not very soluble in water) can be collected in the inverted test tube.

❷ The brown fumes enter the U-tube, which is kept in an ice bath. Here you can see that the fumes are a mixture of gases. The tube has been temporarily taken out of the ice bath for this picture. The brown fumes are nitrogen dioxide, NO_2, one of the main smog gases. The green liquid that has condensed out as the nitrogen dioxide is cooled contains N_2O_4, a yellow liquid which in this case is contaminated by a blue impurity, possibly N_2O_3.

❸ The condensed liquid is poured into a flask and then immersed in hot water. Brown nitrogen dioxide fumes are given off.

EQUATION: Decomposition of lead nitrate

Lead nitrate ⇨ lead oxide + nitrogen dioxide + oxygen

$$2Pb(NO_3)_2(s) \Rightarrow 2PbO(s) + 4NO_2(g) + O_2(g)$$

NO_x

The three important gases of nitrogen – nitrous oxide, nitric oxide and nitrogen dioxide – are collectively referred to as NO_x (pronounced "nox").

Nitrous oxide, or laughing gas, is a colorless gas. When it is inhaled, nitrous oxide makes people feel intoxicated (hence the tendency to laugh). It also makes people lose the sensation of pain and then makes them unconscious. Its effects do not last very long. This is why it is used in dental and other minor operations.

Nitrous oxide dissolves in fatty liquids such as cream, so it can be used as the inert propellant in foamed cream.

Nitric oxide is far less pleasant, a colorless gas that reacts on contact with oxygen in the air to produce the brown gas nitrogen dioxide. Nitric oxide is often produced at high temperatures and pressure. One of the most common places for this reaction is inside the cylinder of a motor vehicle.

Nitrogen dioxide can damage the breathing passages of the lungs. The damage often goes undetected until days after the gas is inhaled and then may cause excessive fluid buildup in the lungs.

Nitrogen dioxide is also an important contributor to the production of ozone, which itself has harmful effects. Nitrogen dioxide also contributes to the formation of nitrate particles, another part of smog.

▲ Smog over Los Angeles, California.

Controlling NO_x emissions

It is very difficult to prevent NO_x gases from leaving the exhausts of vehicles because they are a natural product of internal combustion. Some catalysts can reduce nitric oxide emissions by making nitric oxide oxidize carbon monoxide, producing inert nitrogen, carbon dioxide and water. However, the catalytic converter in modern vehicles is extremely expensive.

Also... Smog

Smog is a mixture of gases and small particles suspended in the air. The gases come from power station, factory and vehicle exhausts. The main gas produced is nitrogen dioxide, which is responsible for the brown haze that occurs in the sky over many cities. Local visibility is reduced not by the gases but by small particles in the air, some of them dust and carbon particles, some of them formed as the nitrogen and sulfur gases react to produce sulfates and nitrates.

catalyst: a substance that speeds up a chemical reaction but itself remains unaltered at the end of the reaction.

ozone: a form of oxygen whose molecules contain three atoms of oxygen. Ozone is regarded as a beneficial gas when high in the atmosphere because it blocks ultraviolet rays. It is a harmful gas when breathed in, so low-level ozone that is produced as part of city smog is regarded as a form of pollution. The ozone layer is the uppermost part of the stratosphere.

smog: a mixture of smoke and fog. The term is used to describe city fogs in which there is a large proportion of particulate matter (tiny pieces of carbon from exhausts) and also a high concentration of sulfur and nitrogen gases and probably ozone.

EQUATION: Reaction of nitric oxide and air

Nitric oxide+ oxygen ➪ nitrogen dioxide

$$2NO(g) \quad + \quad O_2(g) \quad ➪ \quad 2NO_2(g)$$

▼ Nitric oxide is a colorless gas that is almost the same density as air. If a gas jar of nitric oxide is put together with a gas jar of air, and the separating cover slip pulled away, the nitric oxide will start to mix with the air (because gas molecules are constantly moving) and oxidize to brown nitrogen dioxide. Because nitrogen dioxide is heavier than air, it starts to sink.

Air
Separating cover
Nitric oxide
Nitrogen dioxide

Nitric acid

Nitric acid (once called *aqua fortis*, or "strong water"), a colorless liquid, is the most important nitrogen acid and has been known about for many centuries. Concentrated nitric acid is an oxidizing chemical. The oxygen it contains is readily given up to other reactants.

Nitric acid attacks all common metals except aluminum and iron. By mixing nitric acid and hydrochloric acid, HCl, to produce a mixture known as *aqua regia*, it is possible to dissolve all metals, including gold and platinum.

In the atmosphere hydrogen and nitrogen combine, given the energy of a lightning flash, to produce ammonia. This in turn combines with rain and becomes available to green plants as dilute nitric acid. Dilute nitric acid can be used by plants as a source of nitrogen fertilizer.

Nitric acid is prepared industrially from ammonia and is used to make a wide variety of compounds, from fertilizers and dyes to explosives.

Preparing nitric acid

This apparatus shows the preparation of fuming nitric acid from concentrated sulfuric acid and potassium nitrate.

Hot fuming nitric acid is incredibly corrosive, so you will notice that all of the laboratory equipment being used is glass (there are no rubber stoppers or tubing, for example).

The fuming gas produced when some nitric acid decomposes at this very high temperature is nitrogen dioxide and water vapor formed together with oxygen.

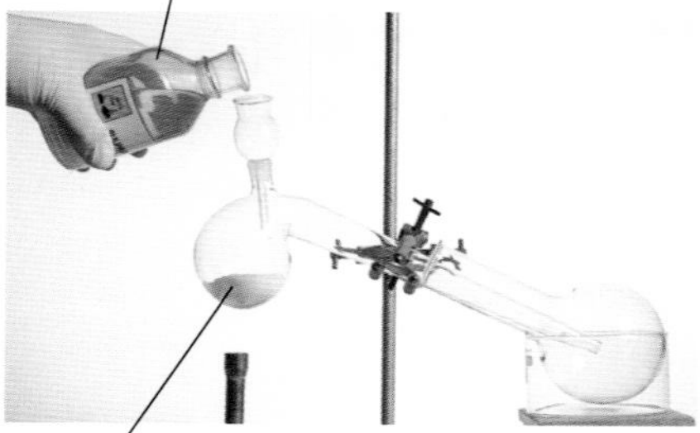

EQUATION: Making fuming nitric acid

Concentrated sulfuric acid + potassium nitrate ➪ nitric acid + potassium hydrogen sulfate

$H_2SO_4(l)$ + $KNO_3(s)$ ➪ $HNO_3(g)$ + $KHSO_4(s)$

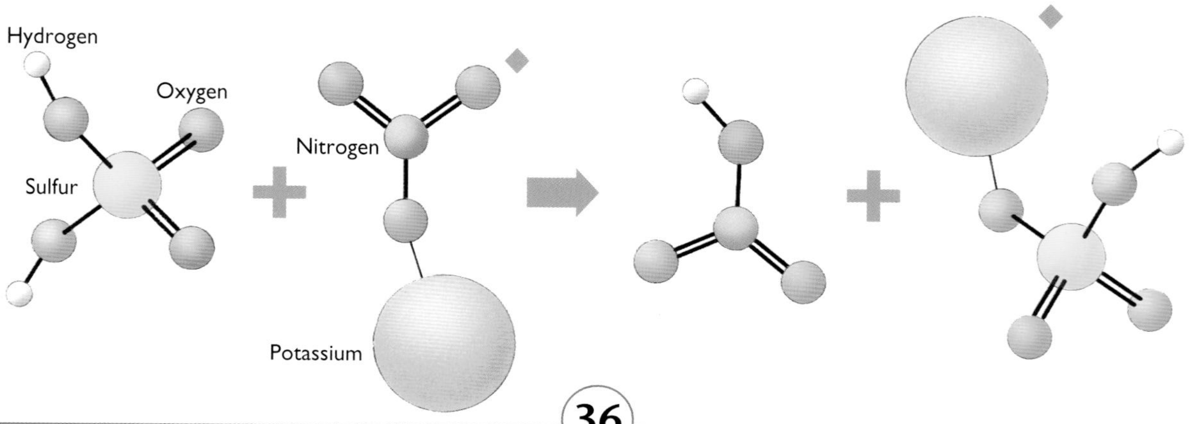

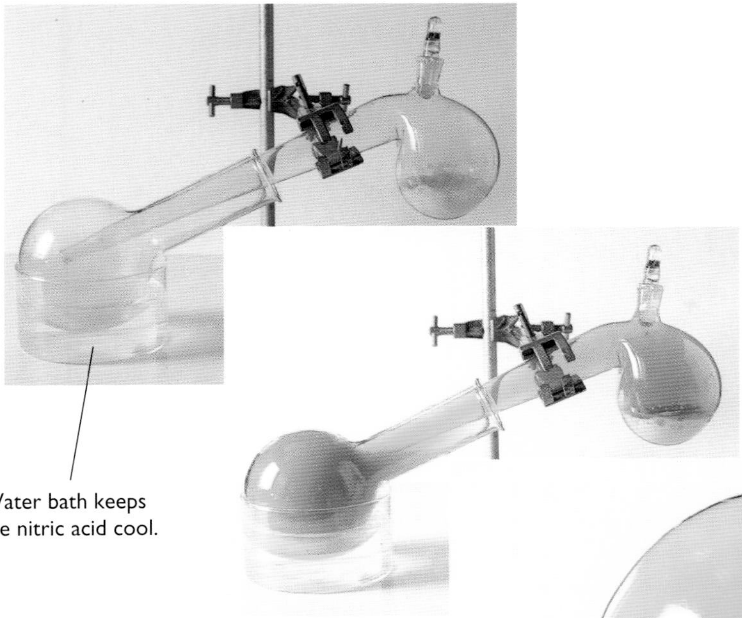

Water bath keeps the nitric acid cool.

fuming: unstable liquid that gives off a gas. Very concentrated acid solutions are often fuming solutions.

oxidizing agent: a substance that removes electrons from another substance (and therefore is itself reduced).

reagent: a starting material for a reaction.

vapor: the gaseous form of a substance that is normally a liquid. For example, water vapor is the gaseous form of liquid water.

Fuming nitric acid

The products of nitric acid

Nitric acid reacts with a wide variety of substances. The reaction oxidizes the other reagent and reduces the nitric acid to a range of products from nitrogen dioxide to ammonia.

Very dilute nitric acid reacts with reactive metals such as magnesium to produce hydrogen and nitric oxide. Less reactive metals such as zinc and iron produce ammonia. Poorly reactive metals such as copper and mercury result in the production of nitric oxide.

Concentrated nitric acid produces nitrogen dioxide instead of nitric oxide. The difference is caused by the fact that concentrated nitric acid is able to oxidize the nitric oxide released, thus forming nitrogen dioxide.

A few metals, such as gold and platinum, are not affected by nitric acid, while others, such as aluminum, do not react because they are protected by their oxide coating.

Also... Making nitric acid industrially

Ammonia (along with oxygen) is used to make nitric acid. However, ammonia and oxygen do not combine easily, and a three-stage process has to be employed.

Stage 1: oxygen and ammonia combine to make nitric oxide (NO). This is achieved at high temperatures and uses a catalyst of platinum gauze. The reaction takes place in less than one-thousandth of a second.

Stage 2: Nitric oxide and oxygen are combined to produce nitrogen dioxide (NO_2).

Stage 3: Nitrogen dioxide is absorbed into water to make nitric acid.

The whole process is called the Ostwald process. It shows that on some occasions, in practical terms what appears to be a rather simple reaction is in fact quite difficult to achieve.

White phosphorus

Phosphorus is a highly reactive element and does not occur uncombined in nature. However, it is widely found in compounds in rocks, especially in light-colored rocks called apatites (like calcium phosphate).

Three main forms of phosphorus are known: white, red and black phosphorus.

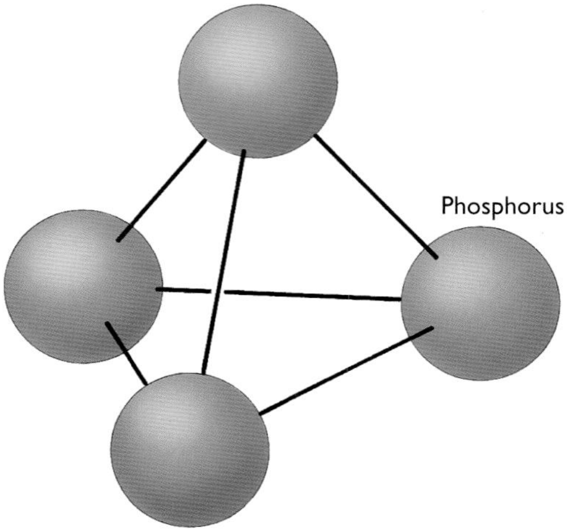

▲▼ White phosphorus. The phosphorus molecule is highly reactive because the bond angle of 60° sets up great strains that can only be reduced by reaction.

White phosphorus

Apatite, sand and carbon react at high temperatures to produce phosphorus and carbon monoxide gases and leave behind a slag of calcium silicate.

Phosphorus gas is collected by condensation and is then made into a soft, white, waxy solid called white phosphorus.

One interesting property of white phosphorus is that it gives out a green glow that can easily be seen in the dark. This is caused by the reaction of phosphorus vapors with air.

White phosphorus can catch fire spontaneously in air and has to be stored under water. The main uses of white phosphorus are for incendiary (fire-starting) bombs, napalm bombs and rat poison.

In the past, white phosphorus was also used for strike-anywhere matches, also called "Lucifers." White phosphorus is highly poisonous, and many people working in the match-making industry used to suffer from "fossy jaw" until safer forms of phosphorus were introduced (see next page). Modern strike-anywhere matches contain a phosphorus compound mixed with a source of oxygen, potassium chlorate. Striking them against a surface heats the mixture, which then reacts and ignites.

Preparing phosphorus

Phosphorus is prepared by heating crushed calcium phosphate rock with coke and sand. This reduces the calcium phosphate to phosphorus.

The phosphorus vapor is then condensed and made into a liquid.

EQUATION: Preparation of phosphorus from calcium phosophate

Calcium phosphate + carbon + silica ⇨ phosphorus vapor + carbon monoxide gas + calcium silicate (slag)

$$Ca_3(PO_4)_2(s) + 5C(s) + 3SiO_2(s) \Rightarrow P_2(g) + 5CO(g) + 3CaSiO_3(s)$$

▼▶ Phosphorus reacts with alkalis, which is an unusual property. When white phosphorus is placed in a sodium hydroxide solution, bubbles of gas form. The gas is (poisonous) phosphine gas (PH_3) that has a fishy smell. Phosphine gas is prepared in the absence of air in this apparatus. The phosphine gas contains an impurity, diphosphine (P_2H_4), which combusts spontaneously in air. This creates the flame you see.

The phosphine gas bubbles catch fire as they burst on the surface of the water. The reaction with the oxygen in the air as it burns forms solid phosphorus oxide and creates white "smoke-rings."

combustion: the special case of oxidization of a substance in which a considerable amount of heat and usually light are given out. Combustion is often referred to as "burning."

spontaneous combustion: the effect of a very reactive material beginning to oxidize very quickly and bursting into flame.

vapor: the gaseous form of a substance that is normally a liquid. For example, water vapor is the gaseous form of liquid water.

"Smoke-ring" of phosphorus oxide

Bubbles of phosphine and diphosphine gas pass through the water and ignite as they burst on reaching the surface.

Concentrated sodium hydroxide

White phosphorus

Red phosphorus

When white phosphorus is heated in the absence of air, it changes to red phosphorus. This is much less reactive than white phosphorus and only bursts into flame when it is heated by friction. The main use of red phosphorus is for safety match heads, tracer bullets, smoke screens and skywriting.

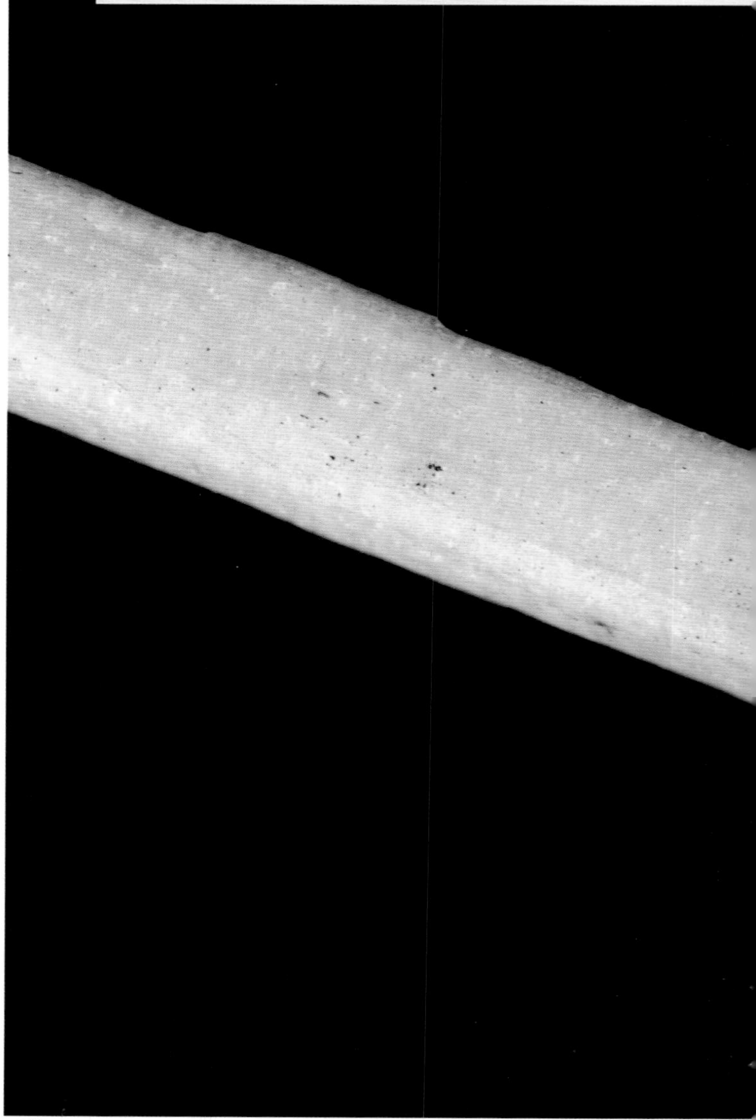

Matches

Matches consist of an incendiary (fire-making) device and a source of fuel, the wood of the match stick. The first matches were tipped with sulfur, but they needed a spark from a flint in a tinder box to light them.

Friction matches – those that ignite simply by being rubbed against a rough surface – were invented in the 1830s. These "strike-anywhere" matches were tipped with mixtures that included the incendiary chemical white phosphorus, which could ignite by spontaneous combustion. These are the matches that will ignite when scraped against any surface. However, many accidents were caused by accidentally scraping them, so today a more stable (and nonpoisonous) chemical containing phosphorus is used.

Safety matches use red phosphorus (on the side of the match box, not in the match head) for ignition. The match head contains potassium chlorate (a source of oxygen). When the match is struck, the head scrapes across the phosphorus on the match box side, causing a small amount of red phosphorus to heat up and come into contact with a source of oxygen. It then reacts and ignites, in turn causing the match head to begin to burn for long enough to ignite the wood of the stick.

◀ Red phosphorus.

▶ The wood provides the fuel for the match.

▼▶ This "strike-anywhere" match contains a mixture of tetraphosphorus trisulfide (P_4S_3) and potassium chlorate ($KClO_3$). "Safety" matches use potassium chlorate in the head of the match and red phosphorus in the striker on the matchbox side. The potassium chlorate provides the oxygen for the reaction.

combustion: the special case of oxidization of a substance in which a considerable amount of heat and usually light are given out. Combustion is often referred to as "burning."

incendiary: a substance designed to cause burning.

spontaneous combustion: the effect of a very reactive material beginning to oxidize very quickly and bursting into flame.

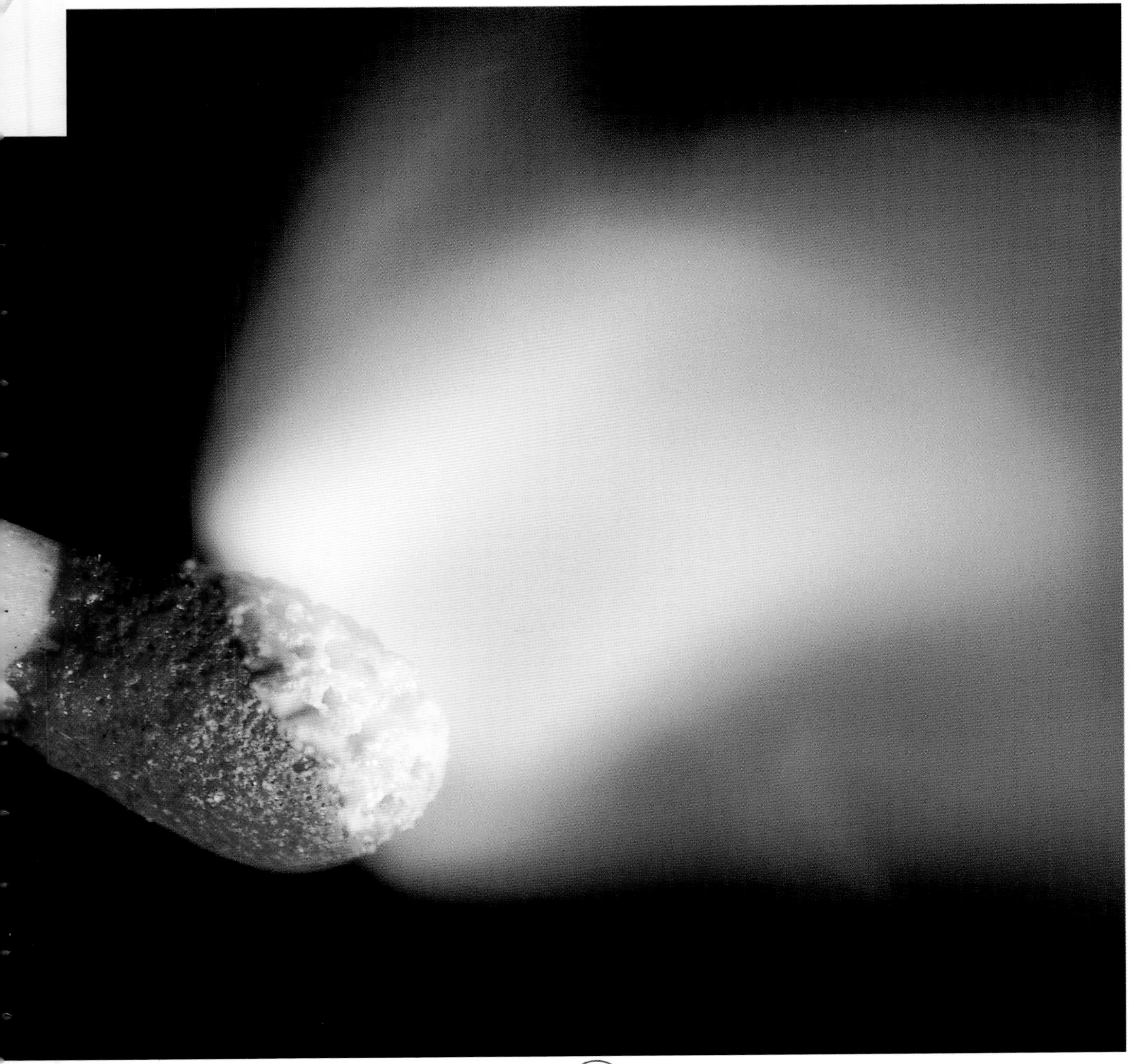

Phosphoric acid and phosphates

Phosphorus, in the form of compounds called phosphates, occurs in all living things. Phosphates play a vital role in allowing both plants and animals to transfer energy.

Calcium phosphate is also important to bone-making, comprising about 1.5 kilograms of every adult human skeleton. Phosphates are also found in the chromosomes involved in reproduction.

Because of its crucial role to life, phosphorus is a key element in fertilizers. Bone meal, crushed animal bones, is a traditional way of returning phosphorus to the soil. The alternative supply is from phosphate rock (apatite), which is mined in Florida and Morocco. This is crushed and treated to produce the fertilizer called superphosphate.

Using phosphoric acids

When phosphoric acid is reacted with bases, a range of useful products results.

When the base contains sodium (as in sodium hydroxide), the resulting salt is trisodium phosphate, used in laundry powders for many years. When reacted with an organic compound, the phosphate is useful as a filler for small cracks.

Phosphoric acid is a hard, glassy solid, the basis of the hard surface for some kinds of enamel.

In very low concentrations phosphoric acid is also used to produce the tart taste in some soft drinks.

EQUATION: Phosphoric acid rust-inhibitor

Phosphoric acid + iron oxide ⇨ iron phosphate + water

$$2H_3PO_4(aq) + Fe_2O_3(s) \Rightarrow 2FePO_4(s) + 3H_2O(aq)$$

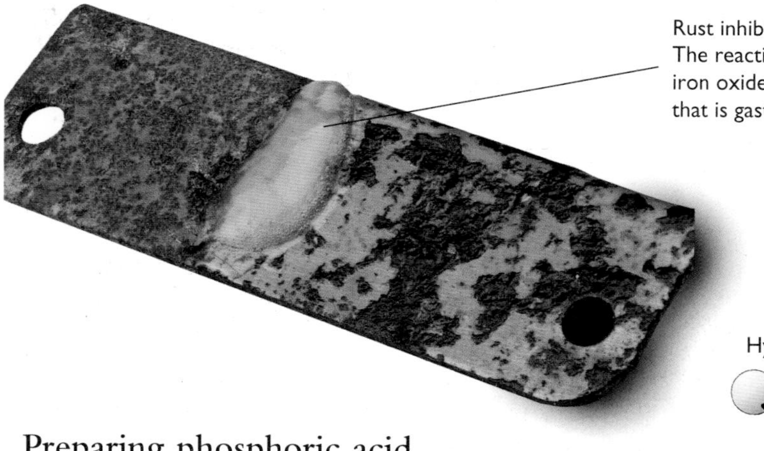

Rust inhibitors are compounds such as phosphoric acid. The reaction between the acid and iron oxide converts the iron oxide layer to iron phosphate, a glassy, insoluble material that is gastight when it dries.

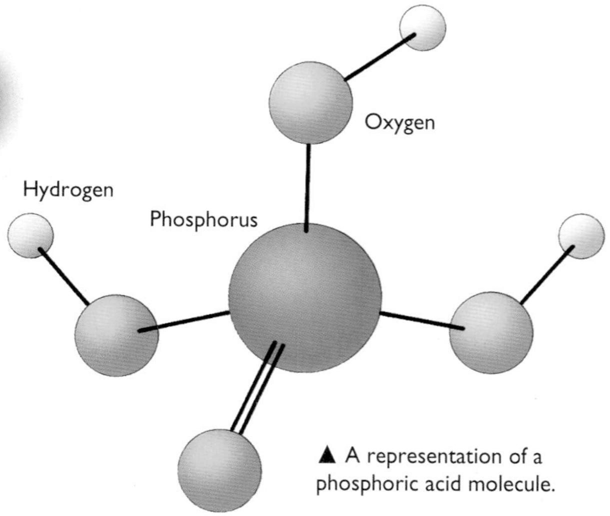

▲ A representation of a phosphoric acid molecule.

Preparing phosphoric acid

Crushed phosphate rock (calcium phosphate) is reacted with sulfuric acid (as in making superphosphate). Further treatment with sulfuric acid and removal of the gypsum precipitate by filtering leaves a 60–70% solution of phosphoric acid.

Superphosphate

This is the most important salt derived from phosphoric acid. In the most common form of preparation, phosphate rock is treated with (inexpensive) sulfuric acid. This produces the products superphosphate and gypsum (calcium sulfate), although as the gypsum has no harmful effects it is not removed.

If calcium phosphate is treated with phosphoric acid instead of sulfuric acid, only superphosphate is produced. This more concentrated form of fertilizer is called double or triple phosphate.

detergent: a chemical based on petroleum that removes dirt.

ion: an atom, or group of atoms, that has gained or lost one or more electrons and so developed an electrical charge.

nutrients: soluble ions that are essential to life.

precipitate: tiny solid particles formed as a result of a chemical reaction between two liquids or gases.

EQUATION: Preparation of superphosphate

Calcium phosphate + sulfuric acid ⇨ calcium phosphate + calcium sulfate

$$Ca_3(PO_4)_2(s) \quad + \quad 2H_2SO_4(l) \quad ⇨ \quad \underbrace{Ca(H_2PO_4)_2(s) \quad + \quad 2Ca(SO)_4(s)}_{\text{superphosphate}}$$

▼ These tablets contain phosphate fertilizers. Superphosphates are used widely in agriculture; but although they are excellent fertilizers, when phosphate-rich waters seep through soils to rivers, they can cause just the same environmental damage that caused the removal of phosphates from detergents.

▼ Phosphates formed the basis of detergents for many years, but they are now less frequently used because of the environmental damage they can do.

Phosphates and pollution

Phosphates are not stored in the soil, so they have to be applied quite frequently. Not all the fertilizer applied is used by plants; some drains away with rainwater and reaches rivers. Here water life, especially algae, make use of the increased supply of phosphate fertilizer by growing vigorously.

Sodium triphosphate has been used in detergents because the phosphate ion acts to stop dirt particles that have been removed by detergents from sticking back onto clothes. As the phosphates are washed away through the drains, they eventually reach water supplies where they, too, act as nutrients for algae.

The combined effects of extra sources of phosphates in the world's natural drainage basins has caused widespread alarm because it causes excessive algal growth (called algal blooms) that take the oxygen from the water they have been growing in and so make life almost impossible for all other water creatures. For this reason, few detergents now contain phosphates. Farm fertilizers seeping to waterways, however, remain a serious pollution problem.

The Periodic Table

Actinium (Ac)	89	Calcium (Ca)	20	Fermium (Fm)	100
Aluminum (Al)	13	Californium (Cf)	98	Fluorine (F)	9
Antimony (Sb)	51	Carbon (C)	6	Francium (Fr)	87
Americium (Am)	95	Cerium (Ce)	58	Gadolinium (Gd)	64
Argon (Ar)	18	Cesium (Cs)	55	Gallium (Ga)	31
Arsenic (As)	33	Chlorine (Cl)	17	Germanium (Ge)	32
Astatine (At)	85	Chromium (Cr)	24	Gold (Au)	79
Barium (Ba)	56	Cobalt (Co)	27	Hafnium (Hf)	72
Berkelium (Bk)	97	Copper (Cu)	29	Hassium (Hs)	108
Beryllium (Be)	4	Curium (Cm)	96	Helium (He)	2
Bismuth (Bi)	83	Dubnium (Db)	105	Holmium (Ho)	67
Bohrium (Bh)	107	Dysprosium (Dy)	66	Hydrogen (H)	1
Boron (B)	5	Einsteinium (Es)	99	Indium (In)	49
Bromine (Br)	35	Erbium (Er)	68	Iodine (I)	53
Cadmium (Cd)	48	Europium (Eu)	63	Iridium (Ir)	77

GROUPS ▶ / PERIODS ▼

Transition metals: groups (3)–(8)

PERIODS	1 (1)	2 (2)	(3)	(4)	(5)	(6)	(7)	(8)
1	1 **H** Hydrogen 1							
2	3 **Li** Lithium 7	4 **Be** Beryllium 9						
3	11 **Na** Sodium 23	12 **Mg** Magnesium 24						
4	19 **K** Potassium 39	20 **Ca** Calcium 40	21 **Sc** Scandium 45	22 **Ti** Titanium 48	23 **V** Vanadium 51	24 **Cr** Chromium 52	25 **Mn** Manganese 55	26 **Fe** Iron 56
5	37 **Rb** Rubidium 85	38 **Sr** Strontium 88	39 **Y** Yttrium 89	40 **Zr** Zirconium 91	41 **Nb** Niobium 93	42 **Mo** Molybdenum 96	43 **Tc** Technetium (99)	44 **Ru** Ruthenium 101
6	55 **Cs** Cesium 133	56 **Ba** Barium 137	71 **Lu** Lutetium 175	72 **Hf** Hafnium 178	73 **Ta** Tantalum 181	74 **W** Tungsten 184	75 **Re** Rhenium 186	76 **Os** Osmium 190
7	87 **Fr** Francium (223)	88 **Ra** Radium (226)	103 **Lr** Lawrencium (260)	104 **Rf** Rutherfordium (261)	105 **Db** Dubnium (262)	106 **Sg** Seaborgium (263)	107 **Bh** Bohrium (262)	108 **Hs** Hassium (265)

Lanthanide series	57 **La** Lanthanum 139	58 **Ce** Cerium 140	59 **Pr** Praseodymium 141	60 **Nd** Neodymium 144
Actinide series	89 **Ac** Actinium (227)	90 **Th** Thorium (232)	91 **Pa** Protactinium (231)	92 **U** Uranium (238)

- Metals
- Metalloids (semimetals)
- Nonmetals
- Inner transition metals

Iron (Fe)	26
Krypton (Kr)	36
Lanthanum (La)	57
Lawrencium (Lr)	103
Lead (Pb)	82
Lithium (Li)	3
Lutetium (Lu)	71
Magnesium (Mg)	12
Manganese (Mn)	25
Meitnerium (Mt)	109
Mendelevium (Md)	101
Mercury (Hg)	80
Molybdenum (Mo)	42
Neodymium (Nd)	60
Neon (Ne)	10
Neptunium (Np)	93
Nickel (Ni)	28
Niobium (Nb)	41
Nitrogen (N)	7
Nobelium (No)	102
Osmium (Os)	76
Oxygen (O)	8
Palladium (Pd)	46
Phosphorus (P)	15
Platinum (Pt)	78
Plutonium (Pu)	94
Polonium (Po)	84
Potassium (K)	19
Praseodymium (Pr)	59
Promethium (Pm)	61
Protactinium (Pa)	91
Radium (Ra)	88
Radon (Rn)	86
Rhenium (Re)	75
Rhodium (Rh)	45
Rubidium (Rb)	37
Ruthenium (Ru)	44
Rutherfordium (Rf)	104
Samarium (Sm)	62
Scandium (Sc)	27
Seaborgium (Sg)	106
Selenium (Se)	34
Silicon (Si)	14
Silver (Ag)	47
Sodium (Na)	11
Strontium (Sr)	38
Sulfur (S)	16
Tantalum (Ta)	73
Technetium (Tc)	43
Tellurium (Te)	52
Terbium (Tb)	65
Thallium (Tl)	81
Thorium (Th)	90
Thulium (Tm)	69
Tin (Sn)	50
Titanium (Ti)	22
Tungsten (W)	74
Ununbium (Uub)	112
Ununhexium (Uuh)	116
Ununnilium (Uun)	110
Ununoctium (Uuo)	118
Ununquadium (Uuq)	114
Unununium (Uuu)	111
Uranium (U)	92
Vanadium (V)	23
Xenon (Xe)	54
Ytterbium (Yb)	70
Yttrium (Y)	39
Zinc (Zn)	30
Zirconium (Zr)	40

(9)	(10)	(11)	(12)	3 (13)	4 (14)	5 (15)	6 (16)	7 (17)	8 or 0 (18)
									2 He Helium 4
				5 B Boron 11	6 C Carbon 12	7 N Nitrogen 14	8 O Oxygen 16	9 F Fluorine 19	10 Ne Neon 20
				13 Al Aluminum 27	14 Si Silicon 28	15 P Phosphorus 31	16 S Sulfur 32	17 Cl Chlorine 35	18 Ar Argon 40
27 Co Cobalt 59	28 Ni Nickel 59	29 Cu Copper 64	30 Zn Zinc 65	31 Ga Gallium 70	32 Ge Germanium 73	33 As Arsenic 75	34 Se Selenium 79	35 Br Bromine 80	36 Kr Krypton 84
45 Rh Rhodium 103	46 Pd Palladium 106	47 Ag Silver 108	48 Cd Cadmium 112	49 In Indium 115	50 Sn Tin 119	51 Sb Antimony 122	52 Te Tellurium 128	53 I Iodine 127	54 Xe Xenon 131
77 Ir Iridium 192	78 Pt Platinum 195	79 Au Gold 197	80 Hg Mercury 201	81 Tl Thallium 204	82 Pb Lead 207	83 Bi Bismuth 209	84 Po Polonium (209)	85 At Astatine (210)	86 Rn Radon (222)
109 Mt Meitnerium (266)	110 Uun Ununnilium (272)	111 Uuu Unununium (272)	112 Uub Ununbium (277)		114 Uuq Ununquadium (289)		116 Uuh Ununhexium (289)		118 Uuo Ununoctium (293)

61 Pm Promethium (145)	62 Sm Samarium 150	63 Eu Europium 152	64 Gd Gadolinium 157	65 Tb Terbium 159	66 Dy Dysprosium 163	67 Ho Holmium 165	68 Er Erbium 167	69 Tm Thulium 169	70 Yb Ytterbium 173
93 Np Neptunium (237)	94 Pu Plutonium (244)	95 Am Americium (243)	96 Cm Curium (247)	97 Bk Berkelium (247)	98 Cf Californium (251)	99 Es Einsteinium (252)	100 Fm Fermium (257)	101 Md Mendelevium (258)	102 No Nobelium (259)

Understanding equations

As you read through Volumes 1 to 15 in the Elements set, you will notice that many pages contain equations using symbols. Symbols make it easy for chemists to write out the reactions that are occurring in a way that allows a better understanding of the processes involved. If you are not familiar with these symbols, these pages explain them.

Symbols for the elements

The basis for the modern use of symbols for elements dates back to the 19th century. At that time a shorthand was developed using the first letter of the element wherever possible. Thus O stands for oxygen, H stands for hydrogen, and so on. However, if we were to use only the first letter, there could be some confusion. For example, nitrogen and nickel would both use the symbols N. To overcome this problem, many element symbols take the first two letters of the full name, with the second letter in lowercase. So, although nitrogen is N, nickel becomes Ni. Not all symbols come from the English name; many use the Latin name instead. That is why, for example, gold is not G but Au (from the Latin *aurum*), and sodium has the symbol Na (from the Latin *natrium*).

Compounds of elements are made by combining letters. So, the molecule carbon

Written and symbolic equations

In this book important chemical equations are briefly stated in words (they are called word equations) and are then shown in their symbolic form along with the states.

What reaction the equation illustrates

EQUATION: The formation of calcium hydroxide

Word equation — *Calcium oxide + water ➪ calcium hydroxide*

Symbol equation — $CaO(s) + H_2O(l) ➪ Ca(OH)_2(aq)$

heated

Sometimes you will find additional descriptions below the symbolic equation.

Symbol showing the state: *s* is for solid, *l* is for liquid, *g* is for gas, and *aq* is for aqueous.

Diagrams

Some of the equations are shown as graphic representations.

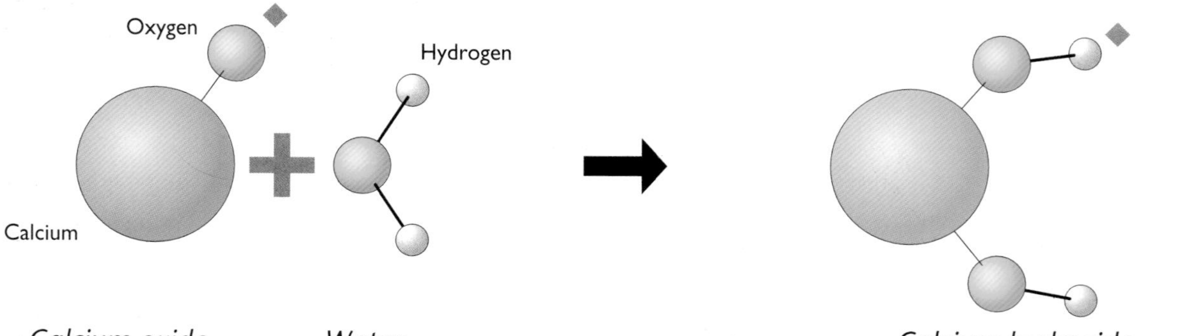
Oxygen
Hydrogen
Calcium

Calcium oxide *Water* *Calcium hydroxide*

Sometimes the written equation is broken up and put below the relevant stages in the graphic representation.

monoxide is CO. By using lowercase letters for the second letter of an element, it is possible to show that cobalt, symbol Co, is not the same as the molecule carbon monoxide, CO.

However, the letters can be made to do much more than this. In many molecules atoms combine in unequal numbers. So, for example, carbon dioxide has one atom of carbon for every two of oxygen. That is shown by using the number 2 beside the oxygen, and the symbol becomes CO_2.

In practice some groups of atoms combine as a unit with other substances. Thus, for example, calcium bicarbonate (one of the compounds used in some antacid pills) is written $Ca(HCO_3)_2$. This shows that the part of the substance inside the parentheses reacts as a unit, and the 2 outside the parentheses shows the presence of two such units.

Some substances attract water molecules to themselves. To show this, a dot is used. So, the blue form of copper sulfate is written $CuSO_4.5H_2O$. In this case five molecules of water attract to one of copper sulfate. When you see the dot, you know that this water can be driven off by heating; it is part of the crystal structure.

In a reaction substances change by rearranging the combinations of atoms. The way they change is shown by using the chemical symbols, placing those that will react (the starting materials, or reactants) on the left and the products of the reaction on the right. Between the two an arrow shows which way the reaction is going.

It is possible to describe a reaction in words. That produces word equations, which are given throughout Volumes 1 to 15. However, it is easier to understand what is happening by using an equation containing symbols. They are also given in many places. They are not shown when the equations are very complex.

In any equation both sides balance; that is, there must be an equal number of like atoms on both sides of the arrow. When you try to write down reactions, you, too, must balance your equation; you cannot have a few atoms left over at the end!

The symbols in parentheses are abbreviations for the physical state of each substance taking part, so that (*s*) is used for solid, (*l*) for liquid, (*g*) for gas, and (*aq*) for an aqueous solution, that is, a solution of a substance dissolved in water.

Atoms and ions
Each sphere represents a particle of an element. A particle can be an atom or an ion. Each atom or ion is associated with other atoms or ions through bonds – forces of attraction. The size of the particles and the nature of the bonds can be extremely important in determining the nature of the reaction or the properties of the compound.

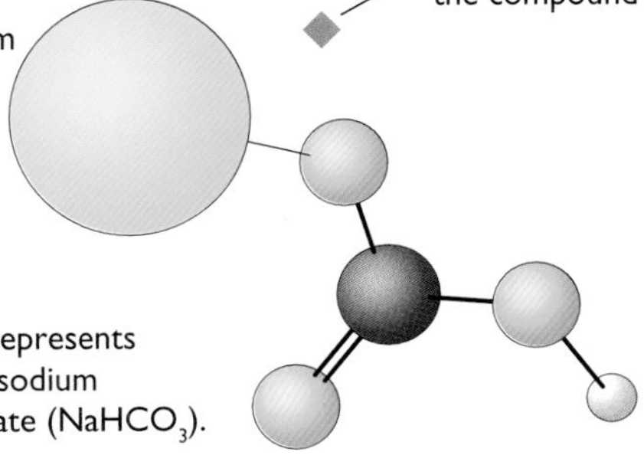
This symbol indicates that the compound is ionic.
Sodium

▶ This represents a unit of sodium bicarbonate ($NaHCO_3$).

The term "unit" is sometimes used to simplify the representation of a combination of ions.

Chemical symbols, equations, and diagrams
The arrangement of any molecule or compound can be shown in one of the two ways shown below, depending on which gives the clearer picture. The left-hand image is called a ball-and-stick diagram because it uses rods and spheres to show the structure of the material. This example shows water, H_2O. There are two hydrogen atoms and one oxygen atom.

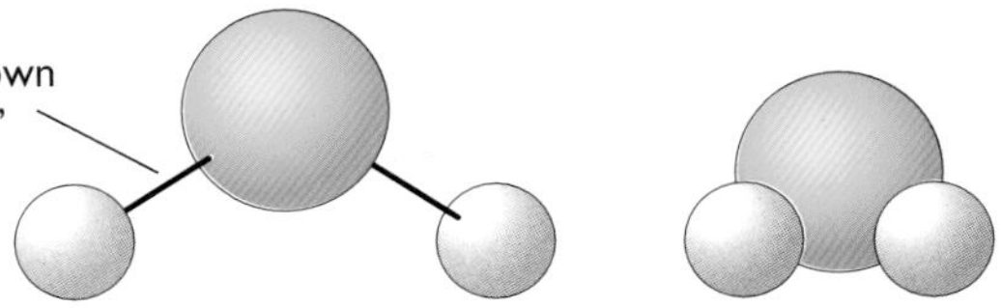
Bond shown by "stick"

Colors too
The colors of each of the particles help differentiate the elements involved. The diagram can then be matched to the written and symbolic equation given with the diagram. In the case above, oxygen is red, and hydrogen is gray.

Key facts about...

Name: nitrogen
Symbol: N
Atomic number: 7
Atomic weight: 14.01
Position in Periodic Table: group 5 (15) (nitrogen group); period 2
State at room temperature: gas
Color: colorless
Density of gas at 20°C: 1.17 g/l
Melting point: -209.86°C
Boiling point: -196°C
Origin of name: the French chemist Antoine Lavoisier named it *azote* because no living thing could survive in it (from the Greek word meaning life). This term is still used in French. The name nitrogen was coined in 1790 after a common mineral then known as niter (potassium nitrate) from *niter* and *-gen*, meaning niter-forming.
Shell pattern of electrons: 2–5
Further facts on this element can be found in Volume 17: Francium to Polonium

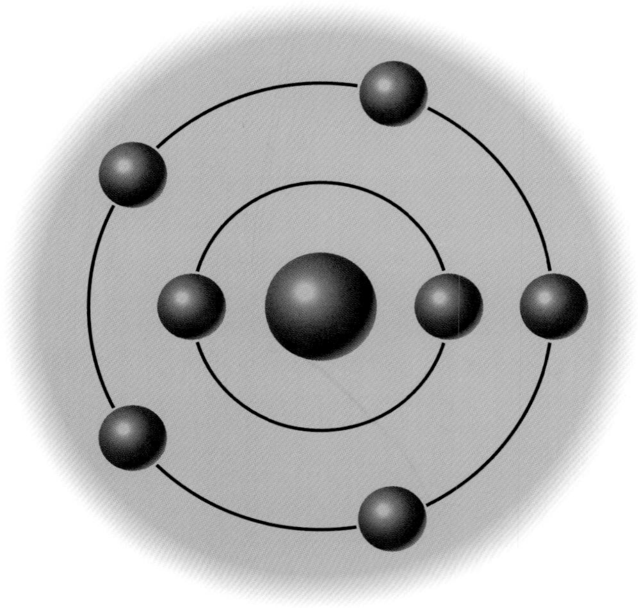

Name: phosphorus
Symbol: P
Atomic number: 15
Atomic weight: 30.97
Position in Periodic Table: group 5 (15) (nitrogen group); period 3
State at room temperature: solid
Color: colorless, white, red, black
Density of solid: 1.82 g/cc (white)
Melting point: 44.2°C (white)
Boiling point: 280°C (white)
Origin of name: from the Greek word *phosphoros*, meaning bringer of light
Shell pattern of electrons: 2–8–5
Further facts on this element can be found in Volume 17: Francium to Polonium

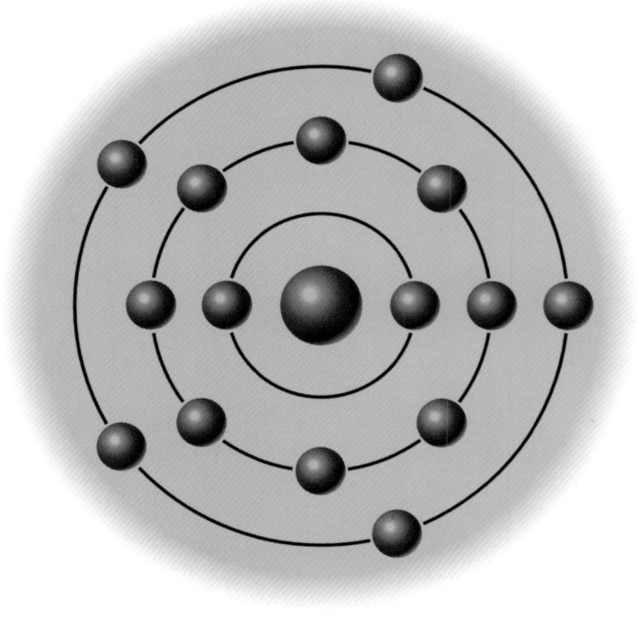

Glossary of technical terms

acid rain: rain that is contaminated by acid gases such as sulfur dioxide and nitrogen oxides released by pollution.

alkaline: the opposite of acidic. Alkalis are bases that dissolve, and alkaline materials are called basic materials. Solutions of alkalis have a pH greater than 7.0 because they contain relatively few hydrogen ions.

antioxidant: a substance that prevents oxidation of some other substance.

catalyst: a substance that speeds up a chemical reaction but itself remains unaltered at the end of the reaction.

combustion: the special case of oxidization of a substance in which a considerable amount of heat and usually light are given out. Combustion is often referred to as "burning."

decompose: to break down a substance (for example, by heat or with the aid of a catalyst) into simpler components. In such a chemical reaction only one substance is involved.

detergent: a chemical based on petroleum that removes dirt.

dissolve: to break down a substance in a solution without reacting.

explosive: a substance which, when a shock is applied to it, decomposes very rapidly, releasing a very large amount of heat and creating a large volume of gases as a shock wave.

fixing: a term applied especially to nitrogen to describe the way that the gas nitrogen can be made into solid and liquid nitrogen-containing compounds that can be used as fertilizers.

fuming: unstable liquid that gives off a gas. Very concentrated acid solutions are often fuming solutions.

incendiary: a substance designed to cause burning.

ion: an atom, or group of atoms, that has gained or lost one or more electrons and so developed an electrical charge. Ions behave differently from electrically neutral atoms and molecules. They can move in an electric field, and they can also bind strongly to solvent molecules such as water. Positively charged ions are called cations; negatively charged ions are called anions. Ions carry electrical current through solutions.

isotopes: atoms that have the same number of protons in their nucleus, but which have different masses; for example, carbon-12 and carbon-14.

nutrients: soluble ions that are essential to life.

oxidizing agent: a substance that removes electrons from another substance (and therefore is itself reduced).

ozone: a form of oxygen whose molecules contain three atoms of oxygen. Ozone is regarded as a beneficial gas when high in the atmosphere because it blocks ultraviolet rays. It is a harmful gas when breathed in, so low-level ozone that is produced as part of city smog is regarded as a form of pollution. The ozone layer is the uppermost part of the stratosphere.

precipitate: tiny solid particles formed as a result of a chemical reaction between two liquids or gases.

radioactive: emitting radiation or particles from the nucleus of its atoms.

reagent: a starting material for a reaction.

resin: resins are natural or synthetic polymers. They can be molded into solid objects or spun into thread.

smog: a mixture of smoke and fog. The term is used to describe city fogs in which there is a large proportion of particulate matter (tiny pieces of carbon from exhausts) and also a high concentration of sulfur and nitrogen gases and probably ozone.

soluble: a substance that will readily dissolve in a solvent.

spontaneous combustion: the effect of a very reactive material beginning to oxidize very quickly and bursting into flame.

vapor: the gaseous form of a substance that is normally a liquid. For example, water vapor is the gaseous form of liquid water.

volatile: readily forms a gas.

Set Index

USING THE SET INDEX

The 18 volumes in the *Elements* set are:

Volume Number	*Title*
1.	Hydrogen and the Noble Gases
2.	Sodium and Potassium
3.	Calcium and Magnesium
4.	Iron, Chromium, and Manganese
5.	Copper, Silver, and Gold
6.	Zinc, Cadmium, and Mercury
7.	Aluminum
8.	Carbon
9.	Silicon
10.	Lead and Tin
11.	Nitrogen and Phosphorus
12.	Oxygen
13.	Sulfur
14.	Chlorine, Fluorine, Bromine, and Iodine
15.	Uranium and Other Radioactive Elements
16.	Actinium to Fluorine
17.	Francium to Polonium
18.	Potassium to Zirconium

An example entry:

Index entries are listed alphabetically. Volume numbers are in bold and are followed by page references in roman.

sodium (Na) **See Vol. 2 and Vol. 18:** 24–25; **1:** 36, **7:** 6, **9:** 11, 24, 38

In this case sodium gets extensive coverage in Volume 2: Sodium and Potassium and on pages 24 and 25 of Volume 18: Potassium to Zirconium. Sodium is also discussed on page 36 of Volume 1, page 6 of Volume 7, and pages 11, 24, and 38 of Volume 9.

A

B

C

D

E

F

G

H

Q

R

S

T

U

V

W

X

Y

Z